D1083834

RELIGION AND PHILOSOPHY

Other works by Frederick C. Copleston

Nietzsche, London 1942

Arthur Schopenhauer, London 1946

A History of Philosophy, 8 Vols., London 1946–66

Aquinas, London 1955

Contemporary Philosophy, London 1956, revised ed. 1972

A History of Medieval Philosophy, London 1972

Frederick C. Copleston, SJ

RELIGION AND
PHILOSOPHY

BOOKS
10 East 53d St., New York 10022
(a division of Harper & Row Publishers, Inc.)

Published in the U.S.A. 1974 by
HARPER & ROW PUBLISHERS, INC.
BARNES AND NOBLE IMPORT DIVISION

First published in 1974 by
Gill and Macmillan Ltd.
2 Belvedere Place
Dublin 1, Ireland
and in London through
association with the
Macmillan Group of Publishing Companies

Jacket design by Hilliard Hayden

ISBN 06 491282 5

Printed in Northern Ireland by W. & G. Baird Ltd.

Contents

Introduction

THE first five chapters of this book represent five of the six lectures which I gave in 1969 in the University of Dundee, whereas chapters six to ten are reprints of articles which originally appeared in the *Heythrop Journal* in 1960–61. The natural chronological order is thus reversed. There is however a good reason for this procedure. The Dundee lectures were intended for a general audience, not simply for students of philosophy. They touched on a variety of topics connected with the relations between philosophy and religion; and no particular theme could be developed at length. On the printed programme the first lecture was advertised as treating of 'metaphysics as embodying a religious impulse'; and in the course of it I referred in passing to the articles in the *Heythrop Journal* as expressing a certain view of 'transcendent metaphysics', namely as the human spirit's attempt to appropriate in reflection its own orientation to the Godhead. It is true that I gave to the articles a common and general title, 'Man and Metaphysics'. But they constituted a continuous reflection on a particular theme of a more limited nature than the variety of subjects touched on in the Dundee lectures. Thus even though the articles were written some years before the Dundee lectures, it seems appropriate that in the present volume they should be placed after the lectures.

In regard to the Dundee lectures, my position is still substantially the same as it was when I gave them. It is natural enough that theologians should reject any view of the function and scope of philosophy which implies that Christian faith is logically dependent on previous acceptance of a particular philosophical system. Given the history of philosophy, at any rate of metaphysical philosophy, it is also natural that they should see in philosophy a tendency to convert Christianity

into something else, absolute idealism for example. It is therefore perfectly understandable if a number of theologians welcome the modern attacks on metaphysics which seem to them
to put philosophy in its proper place. At the same time I
cannot share the hostile attitude to philosophy in general, or to
metaphysics in particular, which is shown by some theologians.
For one thing, the idea of autonomous language-games, each
of which can be understood only from within, by those who
actually play the game in question, and which is therefore
immune from all external criticism, seems to me open to
objection. I do not claim that there is nothing in the idea, that
it does not draw attention to points which should be noticed
and borne in mind. But if it is carried to a point at which any
fruitful dialogue between religious belief and critical philosophy is excluded, theology retreats into a kind of ghetto, cut
off from the cultural life of which philosophy is one expression.
It is all very well to claim that faith is the response to God's
self-disclosure or self-revelation, and that philosophy does not
enter into the matter at all. I have no wish to deny that faith
is such a response. But unless a policy of complete silence is
observed, the disclosure or revelation must be expressed. It
cannot even be thought without internal expression. And once
it is expressed, there is room for dialogue between the theologian
and the philosopher. If the former claims that what he says
cannot be understood except by an esoteric circle and that a
philosopher's comments are necessarily irrelevant, his claim has
questionable implications in regard to linguistic theory. As for
metaphysics, I cannot agree that it is, in itself, either impious or
a threat to religion. For it can (not necessarily does) embody a
genuinely religious impulse, a movement towards the ultimate
reality. To be sure, metaphysical philosophy can set itself up as
a rival to theology or try to absorb theology within itself; and
by selecting appropriate examples we can give a cash-value to
the idea of an irreconcilable clash between the God of the
philosophers and the God of religion. But in my opinion the
trouble lies not with metaphysics as such but with an exaggerated conception of the scope and power of metaphysics.
Limitation of this scope and power must however be the result
of philosophy's critical self-reflection, not of dogmatic pro-
nouncements from outside. The total condemnation of meta-

physics in the name of religious faith seems to me to presuppose a view of the scope of metaphysical philosophy which cannot stand up to critical examination by the philosopher. Finally, I do not believe that theological reflection can be carried on without the making of at any rate implicit ontological assumptions. Quite apart from the question whether or not the existence of God can be proved, belief in God implies, for example, that reality is not confined to what is in principle perceptible by the senses. Conversely, if Christianity is subjected to a radical revision, so that belief in 'supernatural' reality is excluded, the conviction that this sort of revision is necessary seems to have ontological presuppositions. In this case such implications or presuppositions are open to philosophical reflection and discussion.

The articles reprinted from the *Heythrop Journal* can be seen as developing at greater length the view stated in the first of the Dundee lectures, that metaphysics can embody a religious impulse or movement. And I am still in substantial agreement with what I said in them some thirteen years ago. There are however one or two points on which I should like to comment here. In the second of these articles, chapter 7 of this book, I write about the meta-phenomenal and unobjectifiable self in a manner which perhaps tends to give the impression that I am postulating an occult entity hidden away inside. While however I am still convinced that talk about the I-subject is meaningful, I should now wish to emphasise the fact that I regard the I-subject as a function of the human person and not as a distinct entity. Again, in the articles I outline a reductive analysis of the concept of the world, reducing the world to finite things and contingent relations. If it is borne in mind that the objections which I bring against myself in the course of the articles are my own objections, representing what I have described as my *alter ego* or other self, it will be seen that even at the time when I wrote the articles I was none too confident about the validity of this reductive analysis. My doubts remain. On the one hand I am inclined to think that the analysis is defensible and valid, while on the other hand I feel an inclination to say that it will not do. Provided however that it is understood that the articles are not intended as a dogmatic statement of the one true metaphysics but rather as a tentative development of a possible line

Introduction

of thought, I still accept, in substance, the main ideas expressed in them.

Two minor points. In chapter 6 I refer to Professor P. F. Strawson as a prominent member of the younger generation of contemporary British philosophers. For this I apologise to Professor Strawson. He is indeed prominent, a distinguished philosopher; but one would hardly assign him nowadays to 'the younger generation'. My second point is that when I refer in this book to Jean-Paul Sartre, the reference is to the French philosopher as author of *Being and Nothingness* rather than to the writer who has maintained, in the *Critique de la raison dialectique*, that Marxism is the one living philosophy of our age. To be sure, Sartre believes that Marxism has become fossilised and stands in need of rejuvenation through an infusion of existentialism. But he has also maintained that if this rejuvenation were effected, existentialism would have fulfilled its function.

Finally, it will be noted that both in the lectures and in the articles I have suggested that the traditional metaphysical proofs of the existence of God rest on a 'presupposition' or 'initial faith'. If understood in the sense explained in the text, this seems to me quite true. In this case the question arises whether the basic presupposition can be justified and, if so, in what way. In my opinion consideration of this question is much more important than tinkering about with the proofs as explicitly stated.

My thanks are due to the Editor of the *Heythrop Journal* for his kind permission to me to reprint the articles included in the present volume.

Part I

I

The religious character of metaphysics

S o m e philosophers have been convinced that they had fresh news to impart or exciting visions of reality to express. The present writer has no such confidence.

I might of course console myself with the words of Bernard Bosanquet. 'Philosphy can tell you no new facts, and can make no discoveries. All that it can tell you is the significant connection of what you already know.'[1] But whereas Bosanquet was presumably confident that he knew the 'significant connection' between ascertained facts, I should not care to claim that my view of things is undoubtedly correct. And I imagine that a good many of my readers will judge that it is very far from being correct. If what I have to say is judged 'old hat', this will not worry me. General attitudes and patterns of ideas tend to recur. Besides, a general point of view is not necessarily false because it has been proposed before. But I suspect that I may incur the disapproval of both theologians and philosophers, and for much the same reason, namely my attitude to metaphysics.

My general theme is the alleged antithesis between the God of religion and the God of the philosophers. Needless to say, we can easily find particular cases where there is clearly a clash. If, for example, we mean by the God of religion the picture of God given in the Old Testament as issuing commands and instructions and as personally and dramatically intervening in the course of history, this picture is clearly at variance with the representation of God which is to be found in Spinoza's *Ethica more geometrico demonstrata*. But it is idle to think that the problem of the relation between God as conceived in religiously-oriented philosophy and God as conceived in the definite historic monotheistic religions can be settled by simple juxta-positions of opposing concepts. I wish to discuss the matter more generally, though not of course without illustrative examples.

The first point I would like to make, and perhaps to labour, is that metaphysical philosophy can express (I do not say that it necessarily expresses) a genuine religious impulse or orientation of the human mind or spirit. Whether or not this impulse is misdirected or misplaced when it finds expression in meta-physics, is another question. That it can be there seems to me clear.

It is unnecessary to make any apology for discussing meta-physics. My own view of the limitations of metaphysics will, I hope, be clarified in due course. Meanwhile, a good deal of what is said here in the early chapters could be accepted even by those who regard metaphysics as a past episode in the develop-ment of the human mind. That is to say, they can apply it to metaphysics as a historical fact, even if they believe meta-physics is incapable of yielding anything which deserves to be called knowledge.

II

Perhaps I ought to begin by defining some terms, so that we may know where we are. As for 'philosophy', a recent writer remarks that 'a theory of the nature of philosophy is always a philosophical one'.[2] And as I have no wish to narrow the field of discussion in advance by giving a definition of philosophy which expresses a judgement of value, a judgement, that is to say, about what constitutes worthwhile philosophising, I adopt the perhaps rather weak position of saying that I understand by philosophy all that historians of philosophy are accustomed to understand by the term.

What about 'metaphysics'? William of Ockham remarked that to ask 'What is the subject-matter of metaphysics?' is like asking 'Who is king of the whole world?'[3] In both cases there is an erroneous assumption. However, I can say that I understand the term 'metaphysics' widely enough to include both des-criptive and revisionary metaphysics, to use Professor P. F. Strawson's terms,[4] and immanent and transcendent metaphysics, to use the epithets employed by Professor W. H. Walsh.[5]

This leaves us with the term 'religion'. Religion is notoriously difficult to define, definitions varying from those which are rich in content but restricted in application[6] to those which combine vagueness with applicability to all that is customarily called religion. In the West at any rate we ordinarily think of religion as comprising explicit belief in and worship of God or, in the past, the gods. Thus in his notable Gifford lectures Professor C. A. Campbell defines religion in terms of belief 'in the reality of a supernatural being or beings endowed with transcendent power and worth'[7] and of the appropriate attitudes of worship. Original Buddhism would thus be described as an ethical system rather than as a religion. I am inclined, however, to start with a broader concept which will include, for example, Theravada Buddhism. I am therefore prepared to accept the sort of general definition given by Professor Ian G. Barbour. 'Religion, broadly defined', he says, 'is total life-orientation in response to what is deemed worthy of ultimate concern and devotion.'[8] It seems to me that if a man unifies his life in terms of some ultimate ideal which he recognises as having an absolute claim on his allegiance, his attitude is a religious one. After all, even if most people in the West think of religion as unnecessarily including explicit belief in and worship of God, we can also find in quite ordinary utterances the expression of a conviction that a person's attitude to what is for him a matter of ultimate concern is a religious attitude.[9] Further, even if no explicit reference is made to a divine reality, I am inclined to think that recognition of an ethical ideal as having an absolute claim on one's allegiance manifests in some degree that sense of the numinous which Rudolf Otto found at the basis of religion. I have no wish to make a simple identification of morals with religion. But I think that there may come a point at which an ethical attitude passes into a religious attitude without necessarily involving an *explicit* belief in an existing divine reality.

III

Now we would not normally speak of a philosophical system as 'a religion'. For one thing we generally think of a religion as including an element of common cult or worship by a recognisable, self-perpetuating community, an element which does not pertain to a philosophical system.[10] J. S. Mill made a sharp distinction between Auguste Comte's positivist philosophy and his Religion of Humanity, with its proposed cult-system. And Mill was doubtless right to do this. For another thing a religion tends to include some idea of revelation as a source of belief, whereas a philosophical system purports at any rate to be the product simply of man's rational reflection. A follower of Spinoza would not look on the *Ethica more geometrico demonstrata* in the same way in which an orthodox Moslem regards the Koran. Again, just as we think of philosophy of science as presupposing and as not identifiable with science, so we think of philosophy of religion as presupposing and not as identical with religion.

Though, however, a philosophical system would not normally be described as 'a religion', and though philosophy of religion, as an activity of critical reflection, clearly presupposes religion as a datum, there can certainly be such a thing as a religious philosophy. Whatever we may think philosophy *ought* to be— even if we think, with Wittgenstein, that its job is to uncover pieces of 'plain nonsense and bumps which the understanding has got by running its head up against the limit of language'[11]— it is perfectly clear, as a matter of historical fact, that there have been philosophies which can properly be described as religious. The philosophy of Plotinus is an obvious example from the ancient world, while the thought of Karl Jaspers is a modern example. There are also of course the systems of Hindu philosophy.

What do I mean by a religious philosophy? On the more obvious or superficial level we might wish to describe a philosophy as religious in terms of its end-products, in terms, that is to say, of its conclusions or of the theories which it advances, when these bear some resemblance to the doctrines of the great religions. For example, if we consider religion as involving belief in God or the gods, it is obvious that there have been world-views which represented the visible world as manifesting in some way a divine reality, and which included theories about man's relation to the Deity. A case in point is the philosophy of Plotinus. Again, if we consider religion as pro-

viding a total life-orientation, it is obvious that some philosophies have provided frames of reference for unifying one's
life in terms of some pervasive ideal. I suppose that the philosophy of Fichte, with its ideal of the construction and main-
tenance of a moral order on the basis of the physical order,
would be an example.

Obviously, in philosophical world-views ways of life are
associated with metaphysical theories about the nature of
reality. This is clearly the case with Stoicism, Spinozism and the
idealist philosophy of Fichte. But it is equally clear that in
religions such as Christianity, Judaism and Islam, ethical
doctrine is closely associated with religious beliefs relating to
God. This association, whether in metaphysical philosophy or
in a definite religion, gives rise to logical problems about the
relation between ethical statements and statements or beliefs
about what is the case. In other words, the association prompts
discussion of the Humean thesis, no 'ought' from an 'is'. But it is
unnecessary to discuss the subject in the present context. It
seems clear to me that in Christianity, for example, there are
certain inbuilt judgements of value. For example, if someone
claimed to be a Christian but told us that, while he believed
in the doctrines of the Trinity and the Incarnation, he rejected
the Christian ideal of love and regarded hatred as the supreme
value, we would be inclined to tell him that he simply did not
understand what was meant by self-commitment to the
Christian religion. Whether Christian ethical statements can
be deduced from beliefs about the nature of reality is a question
which does not affect the fact that acceptance of certain ethical
ideals is part of Christianity. Similarly, I see no reason why
there should not be inbuilt judgements of vaue in philosophical
systems as well. After all, we are talking about ways of life, not
about metaethics.

It seems evident therefore that as far as doctrines and theories
are concerned, philosophies can overlap with religions. Both
may provide frameworks for life-orientation and doctrines about
God and man's relation to him. And for this reason it is understandable if some theologians are inclined to look on metaphysical systems as rivals to divine revelation and as offering an
ersatz religion. When, however, I speak of religious philosophy
or of religiously-oriented philosophy, I am thinking primarily

B

of the basic impulse or movement of the spirit underlying a philosophy. And I wish to explain what I mean by this.

In his valuable little book on metaphysics Professor W. H. Walsh makes a distinction between transcendent and immanent metaphysics. By transcendent metaphysics he means the sort of philosophy in which the human mind passes beyond the world of sense and claims to relate it to what Kant called the supersensible, to realities or to a reality which is looked upon as being in some sense 'truly real' and as explaining, wholly or in part, the things of our ordinary experience. This idea might apply to the Platonic *eide*; but it would apply much more obviously to God or the Absolute, provided that the Absolute was conceived as in some real sense transcending the Many. Professor Walsh then remarks that if we reflect on the background and interests of transcendent metaphysicians, 'we can see that the practice of religion tends to play a very large part in their lives'.[12] 'Their basic conviction that the familiar world is not the only world'[13] is rightly taken to be demanded by their 'religious practice'.[14]

Now what Professor Walsh actually says suggests the idea of a man who already participates in the worship of a definite religious body, and who then reflects on the ontological or metaphysical implications or presuppositions of his religious practice. But though metaphysics can presuppose adherence to a definite historical religion, such as Christianity or Islam, and indeed it has often done so, it can also express and manifest a religious 'interest' or quest or impulse which is not necessarily bound up with adherence to any form of what might be described as organised religion. A religiously oriented philosophy need not necessarily be an attempt to work out or make explicit the ontological presuppositions of the religious life of a definite community of believers. Still less is it necessarily a form of apologetics, an instrument for defending a given historical religion against hostile criticism. In my opinion at any rate, it can arise out of man's confrontation with or advertence to his existential situation, even if he is not in fact a member of any definite religious community or body.

To say this is to say, I suppose, that I am not prepared to abandon the idea of what is sometimes called the religious premise or religious *a priori*. And I wish to develop this theme a little.

v

It is obvious that every man is in a definite historic situation. He is not, and he cannot be, an external spectator of the world and of history. As the Spanish writer Ortega y Gasset put it, the I and its 'circumstance' go together. It is also obvious, however, that man can take stock of his situation in a way in which, so far as we know, cats and dogs are unable to reflect on their situation. Man can envisage his life as a whole. He can represent it to himself in thought as a totality; and he can raise problems about the overall significance of his life, and indeed of human history in general. He is also capable of giving unity to his life in terms of ideal values or goals which are for him matters of ultimate concern. And he can do this because he is man. Needless to say, I have no intention of claiming that everyone does this as a matter of fact, nor even that everyone feels the need to act in this way. But some people certainly feel the need for a total life-orientation of this sort. And philosophy can be, in part at least, an attempt to fulfil this need by thought.

It has already been made clear that in my opinion religion can be understood in a sense broad enough to include the unification of one's life in terms of ethical ideals or values which are regarded as matters of ultimate concern.[15] To this extent I agree with Professor Charles Morris when he interprets religious discourse as the expression of man's need for a 'focal attitude'[16] which can give a unifying orientation to life. Hence in so far as philosophies have offered overall ways of life, visions of human life and history unified in terms of ideal values or goals, I should regard such philosophies as religious, as fulfilling a religious need or impulse. At any rate I should describe a philosophy of this kind as religious in proportion as the unifying ideal values are felt, from the phenomenological point of view, as having an ultimate or overriding claim on the human will. For it is at this point, I think, that the moral consciousness tends to pass into the religious consciousness.[17]

Now some philosophers would doubtless comment that even if the presentation of a way of life such as I have in mind can be regarded as fulfilling a religious need, we have got past the stage of supposing that it is the business of philosophy to cater for the fulfilment of this need. This sort of thing can be left to moralists, preachers and theologians, while philosophers concern themselves with meta-ethical questions. Moreover, I suppose that a number of theologians would strongly sympathise with such comment, for reasons of their own.

The question of what philosophy ought to be does not, however, concern me at the moment. The fact remains, as it seems to me, that philosophical systems have in the past been inspired by a felt need which can properly be described as religious. Moreover, whether the philosopher is or is not the proper person to meet the need, the need has hardly vanished. Thus it seems pretty clear that even today a good many people feel the need for a new life-orientation and for meaningful goals which can be matters of ultimate concern. This need is based on man himself, on man as existing in a historic situation in which, whether he likes it or not, he has to act in view of end or goals. Hence it seems to me untrue to say that the idea of a religious promise or religious *a priori* is outmoded.

VI

The obvious retort to this is that when people claim that the idea of a religious *a priori* can no longer be maintained, they are not referring to man's capacity for unifying his life in terms of ethical ideals. They are referring to the idea that man is by nature oriented to God or open to the Transcendent, however one wishes to express it. Man certainly has the capacity to look for life-orienting goals. Hence if one means by religion a capacity for unifying one's life in terms of ethical ideals, it is true that man has by nature a capacity for religion. But it is not at all so evident that man is by nature open to the Transcendent or that he needs God. Indeed, this is becoming less and less evident. And this is surely one main reason why transcendent metaphysics is so little practised nowadays. Apart from any logical difficulties, it seems irrelevant.

To say this, however, is tantamount to admitting that at the root of what Professor Walsh calls transcendent metaphysics there does lie a religious impulse or that transcendent metaphysics is the expression of a religious quest. And this is precisely what I am concerned with maintaining. Whether theocentric religion and, with it, transcendent metaphysics are dead or not is another question though an obviously important one. The immediate subject for discussion is the religious character of transcendent metaphysics as a historical phenomenon.

Perhaps one may approach the matter in this way. If we consider the classical metaphysical proofs for the existence of, say, a supreme cause or of an absolutely necessary being, it is obvious to all that they express a movement of the mind towards an ultimate explanation of the existence of finite things. They express, that is to say, a movement of the mind from the Many to the One. What is not so immediately evident, however, is that the existence of the One is in a real sense presupposed. The One is, we may say, the object sought. And the search presupposes that there is something to be found. F. H. Bradley gave expression to this idea when he said that 'philosophy demands, and in the end it rests on, what may fairly be termed faith. It has, we may say, in a sense to presuppose its conclusion in order to prove it'.[18]

The old-fashioned Thomist[19] would probably enter a strong protest. All that is presupposed is the intelligibility of being. And that being is intelligible is shown in every act of knowledge. We have only to reflect on any act of knowledge to see this. What the proofs of God's existence do is to show what intelligibility means, or what it implies, when things are considered under this or that metaphysical aspect. The existence of a One is not assumed from the start. It emerges as the conclusion of a process of demonstrative reasoning.

Nobody of course would deny that the conclusion of a syllogistic argument is precontained in the premises in such a way that to accept the premises involves accepting implicitly the conclusion which follows from them. And if this is all that is meant by the statement that the existence of the One is assumed or presupposed from the start, the statement causes no difficulty.

It is obvious, however, that many philosophers fail to see that the existence of a supreme uncaused cause or of an absolutely necessary being or whatever it may be actually does follow from the premises which are stated by supporters of the argument in question. And if it were simply and solely a question of logic, it should be possible to settle the dispute in a definitive manner. It seems to me, however, that the disputants are sometimes at cross purposes. That is to say, the premises in question, or one of them at least, are not in fact understood in the same way by both parties. For example, even those who object to the use of the word 'contingent' to qualify things and wish to reserve it for propositions must admit that an empirical cash-value, so to speak, can be given to the idea of contingency when applied to things. But they do not admit that recognition of this fact implies the existence of an absolutely necessary being, whereas to some philosophers it seems obvious that it does.[20] And I suggest that a possible reason for this is that philosophers of the second class understand 'contingency' in a metaphysical sense in which it is not understood by philosophers of the first class. That is to say, contingent being is understood, to all intents and purposes, as correlative to necessary being. To admit the premise that there are contingent beings, or that there is a contingent being, is thus to admit from the start that there is a necessary being. The proof simply makes explicit what is precontained in the premises.

Let me put the matter in another way. It seems to me that the transcendent metaphysician really knows where he is going all the time. I am not now referring to those metaphysicians who already adhere to a definite religious faith such as Christianity or Islam and who are deliberately using philosophy as an instrument for defending their faith. For it is obvious to everyone that these philosophers know where they are going, inasmuch as they set out to defend a definite belief. I am referring primarily to philosophers who are not immediately concerned with defending a given historical religious creed or system but who are, so to speak, looking for a One. That is to say, they will not be satisfied with anything else but a One. If in their thought they transcend the visible world, they transcend it towards that which is postulated from the first as the ground of existence of all finite things. The existence of what Paul Tillich sometimes called the 'unconditioned Transcendent' is presupposed from the start or affirmed by an act of what Bradley describes as initial 'faith'.

Words such as 'presuppose', 'presupposition' and 'assumption', however, can give rise to serious misunderstanding. If I speak of a presupposition or assumption, I am not referring to a consciously constructed hypothesis or to an assumption which is made deliberately, as in the case, for instance, of a government which first assumes that another government will act in one way and then that it will act in another way, and which decides on the appropriate steps to take in each case. What I have in mind is something different. And I think that I can perhaps most easily explain it by referring to the philosophy of Karl Jaspers.

Karl Jaspers maintained that man as *Existenz*, man as reaching out towards his possibilities, becomes conscious—or can become conscious—of what Jaspers described as 'limit-situations'. These limit-situations, of which death is one, may be described as the more obvious manifestations of finitude and of what the Scholastics called 'contingency'. Thus man can become aware of the passing and transitory character of finite things, and of the radical insecurity of all human institutions, even of civilisation itself. Jaspers further maintained that serious advertence to or confrontation with the limit-situations is accompanied by an obscure 'awareness' of what he called the Comprehensive, the all-encompassing and all-grounding ultimate unity. 'Awareness', however, is a misleading word in this context. For Jaspers always insisted that the ultimate reality, the One, remains hidden. It is not a thing among things, an object among objects. Rather than say that man becomes 'aware' of the One it is thus more accuracte to say that man, confronted with the limit-situations, transcends them towards an ungraspable goal. This is why it is possible either to affirm or to deny the existence of the One, the divine reality. If it is affirmed, it is affirmed by what Jaspers called 'philosophic faith'. The traditional metaphysical arguments for the existence of God make explicit for reflective thought this basic movement of the mind or spirit; but they cannot compel it. They presuppose and rest on philosophic faith. This is why it is possible for a man to admit the force of, say, Kantian criticism of the arguments and yet feel that there is something in them. For they represent a real act of transcending towards that which eludes man's grasp.

Mention has been made above of the idea of an 'ultimate explanation'. This phrase does not refer of course to an explanation which can be appropriately given in answer to any question, problem, puzzle or conundrum which may be mentioned. It refers to the ultimate ground of existence of all finite things. And, as I have already suggested, the transcendent metaphysician really assumes that there is such an explanation. It may be pointed out to him that if we consider any given thing, we can in principle find the explanation or cause (or causes) of its existence. But it is unlikely that he will be satisfied. For he is looking for something more. And by looking for it he shows clearly enough that he already believes that there is such an ultimate ground of finite existence. This initial belief expresses, it seems to me, an experiencing of finite things, a seeing of finite things if you like, as ontologically dependent on a One which is not itself seen. In other words, I suggest that transcendent metaphysics has as its basis an experience which I should not hesitate to characterise as religious. When I say this, I am of course referring to a transcendent metaphysics which is not simply a repetition of what some philosopher or School has said but which expresses a genuinely personal attitude.

Now if it were simply and solely a matter of looking for a theoretical explanation, it might be objected that there is nothing specifically religious about this exercise. Search for a scientific explanation is not generally thought of as having a religious character. Why should search for an explanation become religious just because it is a question of a metaphysical explanation? To be sure, the ultimate metaphysical explanation of finite existence is customarily described as 'God'. But if God is postulated as an astronomical hypothesis, this is surely bad astronomy rather than a religious act. Is it necessarily a religious act if we postulate a metaphysical ultimate? Perhaps not, but what I have been suggesting is that the search for a metaphysical ultimate, for one ultimate ground of finite existence is based on an experience of limits, coupled with a reaching out towards that which transcends and grounds all limits. And it is possible to see in this act of transcending-towards an expression of the orientation of the human spirit to the divine reality in which, as St Paul puts it, we live and move and have our being.[21]

This is, I think, the sort of experience to which Edward Caird was referring when he spoke of the mind as impelled to seek a unity underlying and grounding the subject-object relationship, a unity of which both subject and object are 'the manifestation', which they presuppose as their beginning and to which they point as their end'.[22] Jaspers of course interprets this experience in terms of his own philosophy of *Existenz*: and for him the subject-object dichotomy is only one of the limit-situations. But Caird and Jaspers seem to be alluding to similar experiences. And Caird finds the foundation of religion in the movement of the mind towards an underlying and all-grounding unity.

Needless to say, I have no intention of suggesting that metaphysics is the only path to God. All that I am claiming is that transcendent metaphysics, when it is the spontaneous expression of a movement of the human spirit, has a religious character. Plotinus said much the same centuries ago, when he mentioned philosophy as one of the paths of ascent to the One.[23] And when Jaspers asserts that proofs of God's existence are 'attempts to express the experience of man's ascent to God in terms of thought'[24] he is saying much the same as Plotinus had said before him.

VII

Now an obvious comment on what I have been saying is that though the sort of experience to which I have been referring doubtless occurs as a psychological event, and though it may sometimes lie at the basis of transcendent metaphysics, it by no means follows that the experience has any cognitive value. It can perfectly well be admitted as a possible psychological occurrence and then explained without one's having to commit oneself to the beliefs which are characteristic of transcendent metaphysics. It may well be true that to interpret metaphysics as due simply to logical or linguistic confusion is inadequate and unconvincing. This explanation will certainly not do for what Professor Walsh calls immanent metaphysics. And even if transcendent metaphysics is apt to involve logical confusion or downright mistakes or fallacies, it seems pretty clear that deep-rooted psychological factors also have a part to play. Even if, however, the roots of transcendent metaphysics may possibly lie deep in the human psyche, this does nothing to show its cognitive value, though it does of course make the persistence of metaphysics more understandable.

Let me take an example. Bertrand Russell has written of the need for 'preserving the seriousness of the religious attitude and its habit of asking ultimate questions'.[25] These 'ultimate questions' presumably arise in confrontation with what Jaspers calls the limit-situations. Indeed, Russell makes this pretty clear by such remarks as that 'we stand on the shore of an ocean, crying to the night and the emptiness'.[26] But though Lord Russell has gone so far as to say that 'I am conscious that human affection is to me at bottom an attempt to escape from the vain search for God'[27] he has repeatedly declared that our desires and emotive attitudes are no sort of reliable guide to the nature of reality. He might be prepared to recognise the kind of experience to which I have referred as a possible psychological occurrence. But he would doubtless regard any conslusions which the transcendent metaphysician would be likely to draw from it as expressions of wishful thinking.

Another example. I do not think that Professor Morris Lazerowitz would have much difficulty in admitting my thesis, that transcendent metaphysics has a religious character. At any rate he sees a relationship between metaphysics and religion, in so far at least as religion involves belief in a divine super-sensible reality. For he says explicitly that 'for many thinkers philosophy, and particularly metaphysical philosophy, is a highly intellectualised substitute for religion.'[28] And he suggests that behind 'the facade of philosophical talk about the super-sensible'[29], there lie the myths of religion. True, a substitute for religion, as Lazerowitz describes metaphysics, is not quite the same thing as religion. But Lazerowitz thinks of the metaphysics of the One or Absolute as expressing 'an important psychological rejection, caused by the unsatisfactoriness of life itself.'[30] That is to say, the metaphysician, in Lazerowitz's opinion, describes the world as 'appearance', and he does so because he finds life unsatisfactory. The world does not measure up to the metaphysician's standard of what it ought to be or of what he would like it to be. He therefore invents another sphere of reality. Presumably Professor Lazerowitz would say much the same about religion, at any rate in so far as religion involves belief in God, in a heaven, and so on.

There is of course another point of view. There are those, for example, who would argue that transcendent metaphysics can be described as the human spirit's attempt to appropriate in reflection its own orientation to the Godhead. Indeed, Part II of this book will be largely concerned with an exposition of this view. It is true that anyone who thinks on these lines has to face the Kantian objection that the idea of an absolute unity as condition of the possibility of all phenomena is a purely 'regulative' idea, and that to draw an ontological conclusion from it is to fall victim to the transcendental illusion. In fact, it may be urged, it involves one in a relapse into the ontological argument, into concluding, that is to say, from the idea of the One to the existence of the One. The reply might be made, however, that it is not a question of a 'mere idea'. Given serious advertence to the limit-situations, the divine reality manifests itself as the attractive but hidden term or goal of a movement, by final causality as an Aristotelian might say. As for the ontological argument, it might be maintained that though, considered as a formal argument, it is invalid, it none the less reflects the fact that in certain contexts at least the idea of God imposes itself on the mind, or that in certain situations God becomes, as Karl Jaspers puts it, 'a natural presence'.[31]

Obviously, those who think on these lines can perfectly well admit that as the term or goal of the movement of the mind which lies at the basis of transcendent metaphysics remains hidden, it is always open to man to conclude that he is grasping at an unreality, a phantom. Indeed, they can hardly fail to admit this. But they can also point out that as the ground of all finite existents cannot itself be a member of the class of things which it grounds, it could not possibly be apprehended as a determinate object, a thing among things. What Tillich called the 'unconditioned Transcendent' must necessarily transcend the sphere of determinate objects.

Such considerations would not of course carry much weight with those who are convinced that psychoanalytic accounts of the experience in question are adequate. But I do not wish to pursue the theme further. From one point of view it is irrelevant to the main theme of this chapter. For though I myself believe in God, what I am concerned with maintaining is that transcendent metaphysics can embody a religious impulse. And this can be admitted of course even by those who refuse cognitive value to religious belief and who offer psychological explanations of both religion and transcendent metaphysics.

VIII

Now in a statement quoted above Professor Lazerowitz speaks of metaphysical philosophy as an 'intellectualised substitute for religion'. And this is, I suppose, the way in which some theologians too regard transcendent metaphysics. It may seem to them an arid and attenuated form of religion. And they may see in it either a rival to true religion, or a half-way house on the road to atheism.

It can hardly be denied, I think, that the statements of some philosophers provide a basis for such evaluation of metaphysics. Bradley, for example, maintained that the concept of God, when rendered consistent and intellectually viable, inevitably passes into the concept of the Absolute, and that with this transformation religion disappears. 'Short of the Absolute', he writes, 'God cannot rest, and having reached the goal, he is lost and religion with him.'[32] Again, we find R. G. Collingwood asserting that 'God and the absolute are not identical but irretrievably distinct.'[33] In my opinion such utterances call for distinctions. Thus a great deal depends on how one understands such terms as 'religion' and 'the Absolute'. But it is clear enough that statements such as those made by Bradley and Collingwood can be used to support the view that there is an antithesis between the God of the philosophers and the God of religion, the God of Abraham, Isaac and Jacob, and that transcendent metaphysics is thus the enemy of religion, even though it often tries to disguise the fact.

This is not, however, a matter which can be profitably discussed until we have had a look at the relations between metaphysical philosophy and the historic religions. I have tended here to treat metaphysics as though it pursued a path of its own in separation from other cultural factors. In point of fact of course it does nothing of the kind. And the relations between transcendent metaphysics and historic religions have been close, though of different kinds. Religion is obviously not the only factor to have influenced metaphysics. But it happens to be the factor with which we are concerned. So in the next chapter I propose to discuss the relations, or some of them, between metaphysics and the historic religions, especially Christianity. This will enable us to get a better understanding of the historic reasons for the hostility shown by some theologians towards transcendent metaphysics. And if I then appear to have involved myself in inconsistency, by first emphasising the religious character of transcendent metaphysics and then citing reasons for regarding it as a menace to religious faith, I hope to make my own position clearer in chapter 3.

2

Metaphysics and the historic religions

BERNARD Bosanquet asserts that 'philosophy depends upon the religious consciousness; the religious consciousness does not depend on philosophy'.[1] I take it that when Bosanquet uses the word 'philosophy' in this context, he is thinking of the philosophy of the Absolute and of the transformation of the concept of God into that of the Absolute. But perhaps we can employ Professor W. H. Walsh's term and say that transcendent metaphysics presupposes the religious consciousness, and not the other way round. This is really what I was maintaining in the last chapter.

What, however, is the religious consciousness? What is meant by the term? We might perhaps substitute 'religious experience', but this term is itself no easier to define. Some writers have tended to equate religious experience with faith. What, they ask, remains of religious experience, if it is divorced from faith? We cannot say, however, that transcendent metaphysics necessarily presupposes Christian faith. For it obviously does not. Plotinus was a transcendent metaphysician. But he was not a Christian. Still, transcendent metaphysics certainly presupposes religious belief of some kind. More generally, metaphysics does not create religion: it presupposes it.

In the last chapter I was concerned with arguing that transcendent metaphysics presupposes and expresses an initial faith in the metaphysician himself, or at any rate that it may and often has done so. But it is obviously not simply a case of the individual philosopher. Metaphysics is pursued in a social milieu; and transcendent metaphysics presupposes religion as a social or historical phenomenon. What is the relation between them?

II

Perhaps we can approach the matter by way of a distinction made by Ortega y Gasset, a distinction between 'ideas' and 'beliefs'.[2] By an idea he meant something which we think and talk about and which we know that we have. If we are asked for our ideas on a certain subject, we may have to say that we have not got any. But if we have them, we know what they are, even if for some reason we are unwilling to divulge them. By a belief Ortega meant an assumption or presupposition on which we count, even if we never advert to it. For instance, that the earth is firm, in spite of occasional earthquakes, is something on which we count. When I step out of the house to go for a walk, I presuppose that the earth will support me. That is to say, I act on this belief, though it is most unlikely that I advert to it.

Now in each culture, according to Ortega, there are a number of beliefs which began as ideas and then became beliefs or presuppositions. They became part of the mental background of the culture in question and were then taken for granted. In each culture there are certain commonly shared beliefs, with which a way of life is associated.

The beliefs which are presupposed by a certain culture or society are not, however, immune from criticism. They can cease to be beliefs and become questioned ideas. And when they have been subjected to widespread criticism, it is necessary for the life of the society that the ensuing state of doubt and uncertainty should be overcome. Otherwise there may result the state of affairs which Nietzsche described as nihilism. It is in such a situation that, according to Ortega, genuine philosophising comes into being. In his opinion, genuine philosophy, as distinct from philosophising as a purely academic pursuit or as an intellectual game, arises out of doubt and uncertainty and out of the felt need for emerging from this state, so that man can live with a framework of convictions, with a recognised purpose and with a set of values. We can doubtless find genuine philosophers in any epoch. But they are most likely to be found at a time when there is widespread questioning of the beliefs and values presupposed or assumed by a culture and which were accepted by a previous generation.[3] The philosopher then attempts to develop a system of ideas to replace the crumbling beliefs.

Now we may be mistrustful of attempts to assign one particular origin to philosophy. Further, we have to remember that if we distinguish between 'genuine' philosophising and philosophy considered as a kind of intellectual game played in universities, we are making a judgement of value.[4] Again, Ortega's distinction between ideas and beliefs stands in need of clarification. A society may share beliefs which are not actually questioned but which are adverted to and are not what R. G. Collingwood described as ultimate or absolute presuppositions. At the same time we can see more or less what Ortega is getting at. And we can at any rate easily think of one historic situation which provides support for his point of view.

It is arguable, for example, that Socrates and Plato endeavoured to give a firm rational basis to moral and religious convictions or beliefs which had been called in question. In the *Laws*[5] Plato asserts that were it not for unbelievers and sceptics, there would be no need for proofs of the existence of the gods. In other words, Plato's natural or philosophical theology presupposed, for instance, Prodicus' naturalistic explanation of religious belief. At the same time, even if Plato set out to provide a rational justification of religious belief, he certainly did not aim at restoring the myths as related by the poets. On the contrary, he sought to purify the popular ideas of the gods and their doings. In a period of intellectual ferment he tried to substitute a system of ideas for the traditional beliefs which had been handed on and which the mentally alert and critical could not accept. To be sure, we cannot draw a sharp distinction between myth and philosophy in the ancient world. For mythical elements persisted. But whereas myth was originally 'truth', the sacred history, for example, of the origins of the world, it was characteristic of the philosophical attitude to have some idea of myth as 'myth'.

In the field of ethics it is clear that Socrates and Plato were opposed to the intellectual revolutionaries who maintained that conventional moral convictions should be thrown overboard. At the same time it is equally clear that they were not content with simply reasserting traditional moral beliefs. They endeavoured to purify and clarify moral concepts and to exhibit clear standards for judgements of value. It is unnecessary to discuss the ontological status attributed by Plato to the Forms or Ideas. It is sufficient to note that he pursued a clarificatory analysis of moral concepts not simply as an intellectual exercise but rather because he believed that it was of great importance for human life and society. Further, Plato's moral ideas were closely connected with his natural theology. For instance, his objections to some of the popular myths were ethical in character.

III

Now when Plato developed a natural theology, he was not trespassing on anyone else's preserve. In the Greek world there was no teaching Church, no defined dogmas, no theologians in our sense of the term, distinct, that is to say, from the philosophers.[6] The emphasis was placed on cult rather than on belief. To be sure cult, unless it is an empty formality, implies or presupposes some belief or beliefs. But it is obvious that in ancient Greece no great emphasis was laid on specific beliefs. It is of course true that some philosophers were accused of impiety. It is always possible for philosophy to be seen as undermining popular religious beliefs or as substituting for them something which does not answer to the demands of the religious consciousness. Apart, however, from the fact that accusations of impiety were sometimes inspired by political rather than by religious motives, Greek philosophical speculation in the sphere of religion, except when it was atheistic, was not a counterblast to established religion. On the contrary, it can be regarded as an attempt to think through in a systematic manner the presuppositions of cult. Cult clearly presupposed the existence of some divine being or beings. And philosophers such as Plato tried to show what should or should not be said about the gods.

Further, in the period when those who were looking for a more spiritual and mystical form of religion than could be found simply in official cults (that is to say, the cult of the city) turned to the mystery-religions, philosophy itself came to offer a doctrine of mysticism. Neoplatonism was doubtless caviar to the multitude. And the intermediary beings of the Neoplatonic hierarchy bore little resemblance to the robustly anthropomorphic deities of the Homeric poems. We may thus feel

c

inclined to regard Neoplatonism and other such religiously-oriented philosophies as a substitute for Greek religion, a philosophical religion for intellectuals. But this was not the way in which the Neoplatonists regarded their philosophy. For they looked on it as preserving the Hellenic spirit and the old religion against Christianity. And unless we propose to exclude from religion the process of reflective thought, it is reasonable to see Neoplatonism and other religiously-oriented philosophies of the ancient world as falling within the process of development of the Greek religious spirit. It is true that philosophising about mysticism is not the same thing as having mystical experience. But the philosophy of Plotinus is certainly inspired by a religious spirit and represents a religious outlook on the world. Further, if Porphyry is to be believed, Plotinus' philosophy of mysticism reflects personal experience on his part. With some philosophers Neoplatonism doubtless became an arid scholasticism. But with Plotinus at any rate it represents an instrument for religion becoming, as it were, conscious of itself in reflective thought.

Speculation by philosophers in the sphere of religious belief was of course generally accompanied by ethical doctrine, by the presentation of a way of life oriented to a goal, whether happiness or tranquillity of soul or virtue or, as in the case of Plotinus, union with the supreme Godhead, the One. But here again, as far as Greek religion was concerned, the philosophers were not trespassing on anyone else's preserve. They were not offering alternatives to some ethical doctrine which was claimed to have been revealed and which was officially taught by an authoritative interpreter of divine revelation. For though there obviously were recognised social duties, there was no officially taught way of life and no authoritative interpreter of revelation.

IV

When we turn to Hinduism, we find indeed commonly venerated sacred texts, the Vedas. But the texts, which were of multiple authorship, were open to different levels of interpretation and themselves provided a point of departure for philosophical theology. For example, although the Vedas postulate a multiplicity of deities, they also exhibit a tendency to imply the existence of an ultimate divine reality which can be named by many names or appear in many forms. Again, though in Hinduism great attention was paid to ritual, there was reflection on the meaning and implications of ritual. And it was the Hindu philosophers who attempted to work out the implications in the field of belief. The philosophers of Hinduism did not construct their systems alongside of or outside or as a substitute for Hindu religion. They stood within the Hindu religion and took its sacred writings as a point of departure.[7] In fact they can be described as theologians, if one so chooses.

This last remark is, I admit, open to objection. As we all know, there were rival traditions or schools. Some philosophers embraced a monism in which the idea of God, as it is ordinarily understood, pretty well disappeared. And it is clearly arguable that to describe such philosophers as theologians is to misdescribe them. There were other thinkers, however, who approximated to theism, especially those who laid emphasis on personal devotion to the Deity, such as makes its appearance in the Gita poems. In any case the various schools had their home within the Hindu religion. In their interpretations and developments of the sacred texts the philosophers were not usurping the place of a dogmatic teaching Church. For there was no such body. The philosophies can be looked at as moments in the development of Hinduism, in the process of Hinduism becoming intellectually self-conscious. We can of course make a distinction between popular and philosophical Hinduism. But this is a distinction within Hinduism, not between Hinduism and a philosophical substitute for it. It is significant that Sankara, himself a monist, recognised that at the level of ordinary experience the view of the Absolute as a personal creator was justified. Philosophical theology penetrates deeper into the truth but there are various levels at which truth can be presented. This point of view seems to be typical of Hinduism. Both popular Hinduism and obscure philosophical speculation can be contained within the same religion.

Obviously, there are limits to the all-embracing character of Hinduism. For there are philosophies which are incompatible with it and which are felt as a threat. But metaphysical philosophy as such seems to be an essential ingredient. When a thinker such as Sri Aurobindo tried to develop Hindu thought in such a way as to overcome the tendency to retreat inwards away from the world of illusion and to introduce a dynamic element, he was acting, we may say, not simply as a philosopher but also as a progressive Hindu theologian. In any case he was a religious thinker, whose philosophy was inspired by religious impulses which proceeded from historic religion—Hinduism and, to some extent, Christianity—and not simply from some vague religiosity peculiar to religiously-oriented philosophers.

These sketchy remarks about Hinduism are, as I am well aware, open to criticism as being a gross over-simplification of something which is extremely complicated. However, I do not think that it will do simply to equate Hindu religion with popular polytheism and to describe the systems of reflective thought as philosophy developed indeed by Hindus but having nothing to do with the Hindu religion. It is doubtless true that some lines of thought represent a psychology combined with a metaphysics the religious character of which is at any rate disputable. In other words, it is arguable that some thinkers did in fact try to substitute a philosophy for religion, as far as the intellectual élite was concerned. But such judgements are apt to reflect the influence of western ideas of what constitutes religion. In any case there was at least one line of metaphysical reflection which envisaged a personal relationship with God. And if we choose to lay the emphasis on this line of thought, we can then see philosophical theology not as destructive of religious attitudes but as promoting religion by going beyond the impersonal Brahman to a personal God.

In general, because of the relation of Hindu philosophy to the sacred texts we can see it as an attempt, or rather series of attempts, to penetrate the truth of the Hindu religion from within. In other words, we can hardly regard the classical Indian philosophies as standing apart from and over against Hinduism in the same way as some western philosophies have stood apart from and over against Christianity.

v

In the case of Christianity the situation was obviously different. In Greece philosophy was to all intents and purposes a native

growth, and it presupposed Greek religion as an already existing historical phenomenon. Similarly, Indian philosophy was a
native growth; and it presupposed a polytheistic religion. The
early Christians, however, found philosophy already in existence. Philosophising had been pursued for some centuries; and
the early Christians found themselves in a world in which there
were various philosophical schools. They had therefore to
adopt an attitude towards philosophy. And it is not surprising
if many Christians took a pretty dim view of it. The early
Christians believed that the way of salvation had been revealed
through Christ. Further, they believed that man could rise to a
new life and fulfil his divine vocation only through incorporation with Christ and through the power of the Holy Spirit. It
was therefore natural enough if they looked on the pagan
philosophers who expounded ways of life and who relied on
intellectual enlightenment and on power of will to lead men to
happiness or virtue or tranquillity of soul as vain talkers, as
men who did not themselves enter into the sheepfold and who
endeavoured to seduce others and prevent them from entering.
It is not simply a question of writers such as Tertullian. We can
find this sort of view even in St Augustine, who had himself
been influenced by Greek philosophy.

As we are all aware, however, another point of view showed
itself. With writers such as Justin Martyr, Clement of Alex-
andria, Origen, Eusebius of Caesarea, we find the notion of
philosophy as the instrument by which the Logos, which
illumines every man who comes in to the world,[8] prepared the
minds of the Gentiles for the gospel of Christ. The Jews were
prepared by the Law and the prophets, the Gentiles by philosophy. The Christian revelation was the fulfilment of both.

Now to a certain extent these two views were quite compatible. For it was obviously possible to look on Greek phil-
sophy in the pre-Christian era as a groping after the light which
finally shone in Christ and at the same time to look on the
philosophical schools existing contemporaneously with Christianity as rivals and as blind leaders of the blind. And this is
doubtless how some Christian writers did interpret the situation. After all, both those who spoke harshly of Greek philosophy and those who took a more favourable view of it regarded
Christianity as the true wisdom, the true 'philosophy'. Both

parties regarded the Christian revelation as superseding autonomous philosophy. Philosophy as the Greeks knew it had fulfilled its historic mission with the Incarnation, just as the Mosiac law had fulfilled its historic mission. Christianity took the place of both. This shared conviction was more fundamental than the difference between those who tended to abuse Greek philosophy and those who tended to pay it compliments. For both thought that it had been superseded, at any rate as far as transcendent metaphysics and the presentation of ways of life were concerned.

Obviously, in the process of faith seeking understanding of itself—in the development, that is to say, of theological reflection—use was made of concepts, or at any rate of terms,[9] taken from the philosophy of the ancient world. But even when we find original philosophising, sometimes of a high order, as with Augustine,[10] it is clearly subordinate to and part of the working-out of a Christian world-view. A distinction was indeed made between what can and what cannot be known without revelation. But the idea of a separate autonomous philosophical system was foreign to the minds of the early Christian writers, who looked on Christianity itself as the true wisdom or philosophy. There could of course be progress in faith's understanding of itself and of its implications; but autonomous systems of transcendent metaphysics and ethical visions had had their day.

VI

At first sight it may appear that the situation underwent a marked change in the course of the Middle Ages. In the early Middle Ages, when philosophy amounted to little more than logic, it was natural to look on it as being, to use a hackneyed phrase, the handmaid of theology. For unless logic is pursued for its own sake, as a formal discipline and at a relatively high level of sophistication, it is naturally regarded as a tool or instrument for use in the development of another science. This is especially true of course when science is thought of as primarily deductive. And as in the Middle Ages theology was esteemed as the chief science, we can understand theologians representing logic as their instrument and mistrusting the antics of the pure dialecticians, who liked to raise problems which they could not solve. When, however, during the later decades of the twelfth century and the first decades of the thirteenth century the Christian West became acquainted with a considerable amount of Greek and Islamic thought and science, a distinction naturally came to be made between philosophy on the one hand and theology or 'sacred doctrine' on the other. A thinker such as Thomas Aquinas lived in a period when the Christian theologians had become much better acquainted with world-views which, as they were obviously well aware, owed nothing to Christianity. As Aquinas thought that the philosophy of Aristotle was in the main true and represented what we might describe as secular knowledge,[11] he had to work out a satisfactory relation between science as the work simply of the human reason and science which took its premises from divine revelation.[12] It may therefore appear that the idea of a separate and autonomous philosophical system, which the early Christians regarded as superseded, had been given fresh life.

We must remember, however, that the leading thinkers of the Middle Ages were for the most part theologians. Bonaventure, Aquinas, Henry of Ghent, Giles of Rome, Duns Scotus, Ockham, were all theologians. And even if a distinction was made between philosophy on the one hand and theology on the other, these theologians had no more intention than had the early Christian writers of developing separate philosophical systems, in the sense of world-views. There is of course a great deal more philosophy in the writings of Aquinas than there is in the writings of, say, St Anselm. And it is doubtless possible to extract a philosophical system, as indeed many Thomists have done. But Aquinas himself was a Christian theologian who was really carrying on the programme of faith seeking understanding of itself, and working out a Christian world-view, using Greek and Islamic thought in the process. It would be a mistake to represent him as concerned with the construction of a philosophical system. To be sure, Aquinas recognised philosophy as an autonomous discipline; and he thought that the philosopher could prove the existence of God. But he also made it clear that in his opinion people would not in fact get very far by philosophy alone either in the knowledge of God or in knowledge of the end or goal of human life.

It would thus be a mistake to think of men such as Aquinas and Duns Scotus as playing two roles, as pursuing theological studies on the one hand and, on the other, developing separate philosophical systems. When separate philosophy is found in the Middle Ages, it is found not so much with the theologians as with, for example, some professors in the Faculty of Arts in Paris. And they tended to represent themselves as exegetes of Aristotle, as historians of philosophy one might say, or, more precisely, as commentators.

At the same time it is obvious that, whatever the personal attitude of the theologians may have been, recognition of philosophy as an intrinsically autonomous discipline prepared the way for the re-emergence of independent philosophical systems. The material for reflection was there, so to speak. Philosophy in the Christian world was growing up. And in the post-medieval world it went its own way, freed from the tutelage of theology or, preferably, no longer subordinate to the priority of Christian faith.

VII

Even during the Middle Ages, however, we can find hints of the view that the God of the philosophers is not the God of the Christian religion. Over-concentration on the thought of Aquinas tends to obscure this aspect of the situation. Aquinas, as everyone knows, says that the existence of God is proved in five ways and then proceeds to give five arguments based on what other writers, Greek, Jewish, Moslem, or Christian, have already said. Further, having proved the existence of a first mover or supreme cause or absolutely necessary being, he adds some such remark as that 'all call this God'. Needless to say, Aquinas did not imagine that the concept of a first unmoved mover was all that Christians meant by God. But he evidently believed that the argument in question proved the existence of a being who is in fact the God of the Christian religion. Some medieval theologians, however, did not believe this. Duns Scotus, for example, not only questioned the validity of the principle on which the argument rested[13] but also made it clear that in his opinion the argument, even if logically watertight, would not prove the existence of the transcendent God of Christian faith.[14] And with William of Ockham the gap between the God of the philosophers and the God of Christian faith tends to widen.

In speaking of Ockham, we must avoid anachronism. For example, to describe him as a logical empiricist in philosophy and a Barthian before Barth in theology is inaccurate on two counts. In the first place, in spite of the empiricist elements in his thought Ockham did not simply reject metaphysics. In the second place, if he limited the competence of philosophy to provide us with knowledge of God, the reasons which he gave were logical rather than theological. That is to say, he wrote as a logician and philosopher, criticising the metaphysical arguments of his predecessors, rather than as a theologian emphasising the effects of the Fall on the human intellect and will.

At the same time, in spite of those historians who try to diminish the differences between Ockham and St Thomas Aquinas, it seems to me that in Ockham's opinion philosophy could not really prove the existence of the one, infinite and transcendent God of the Christian religion.[15] Further it is clear that Ockham thought of Graeco-Islamic metaphysics as tending to limit the divine freedom by representing creation as a necessary process of emanation, whereas the absolute freedom of the divine will was essential to the Christian idea of God.

Insistence on the divine freedom and omnipotence was also a prominent feature of Ockham's ethical outlook. He would have nothing to do with the idea of an impersonal moral law or of absolute values, subsisting in some mysterious way and governing even the will of God. On the contrary, right and wrong, good and bad, depended, in Ockham's view, on the divine will. Anything that God commanded was right: anything that he forbade was wrong and evil.

This point of view is open to misunderstanding. According to Ockham God could issue any command which was not self-contradictory. And this suggests that for him the moral law depends simply and solely on the arbitrary or capricious will of God. When, however, Ockham said that God could command anything which did not involve a contradiction, he was speaking of logical possibility and he was considering God as absolute power. In point of fact he was obviously well aware that Christians do not conceive God simply as absolute power. The will of God, we may say, is the absolutely good or holy will. Hence whatever action is commanded by God must be right.

It is certainly not my intention to suggest that Ockham's

ethical theory is immune from criticism. The point to notice, however, is that it reflects, and was doubtless thought of by Ockham as reflecting, the moral consciousness of the devout Christian believer. That is to say, the devout Christian is concerned with doing the will of God or what he believes to be the will of God.[16] And wrong action is for him 'sin'. From the logical point of view Ockham may have looked on ethical precepts or laws as commands and have concluded that they must therefore emanate from a will. His theory had a logical aspect. At the same time he was laying emphasis on a Christian theocentric ethics as distinct from some purely philosophical ethics. It seemed obvious to him that the supreme moral rule was to obey God, to do the divine will, which was the same as loving God.

There is therefore truth in Professor Etienne Gilson's remark that 'the God in whom Ockham believes is Yahweh, who obeys nothing, not even Ideas'.[17] Even if Ockham gives his attention to logical criticism of the metaphysical arguments of his predecessors rather than to emphasising the effects of the Fall, it seems clear to me that as a theologian he is eager to free Christian faith from what he regards as the contamination of Graeco-Islamic metaphysics. We can find of course something of the same kind in medieval Islam, with the groups of Moslem theologians who strongly disapproved of the 'rationalism' of some of the leading Islamic philosophers.

VIII

As we have noticed, the leading philosophers of the Middle Ages were for the most part theologians.[18] And as they all had an idea of divine revelation given through Christ and mediated by the Church, they naturally set limits to the scope of philosophy in the sphere of religious belief. This is true of Aquinas, even if he had more confidence in the cognitive reach of metaphysics than was shown by some of his successors. If, however, we regard metaphysics as a sustained attempt to understand reality, to obtain conceptual mastery over it, metaphysics, left to itself, naturally tries to understand the whole of reality, so far as this is possible. The metaphysician, if he has any sense, recognises that the human mind has its limitations. But when philosophy is set free from subordination to theological interests and convictions and becomes autonomous in fact, metaphysicians naturally tend to regard the sphere of the knowable as coterminous with what can be known by science and philosophy. They do not take kindly to limitations set by ecclesiastical authority or by theologians. After the Middle Ages therefore we find a succession of world-views, some of which at any rate are clearly at variance with Christian belief and may be accompanied by ideas of human life and its goal which differ in varying degrees from the Christian vision of man and his life.

There is no difficulty therefore in understanding theologians coming to view metaphysics as a rival. For it has often professed to answer the so-called 'ultimate questions' which the Christian religion claims to answer. It is no matter of surprise then if a number of theologians have rejoiced in what they regard as the downfall of metaphysics. If scientists can be prevented from taking the place of metaphysicians and producing world-views, the field is left open for faith to present its vision.

With an open enemy, however, or with an open and declared rival, we know where we are. Everything is above-board. What is particularly obnoxious about metaphysics, from the point of view of some orthodox theologians, is the tendency which it has sometimes shown to start, as it were, from within the sphere of religion and then to transform the concept of the personal God of Judaeo-Christian religion into something else or to substitute alleged knowledge for faith. For then metaphysics appears as an enemy in disguise, an enemy who, in effect, undermines religious faith from within. If a metaphysician expounds, for instance, a dogmatic materialism, everyone sees at once that his system is incompatible with traditional Christianity or Judaism. There is no need to labour the point. But if he starts, as it were, with faith and then holds out the promise of a knowledge which is higher than faith, he is far more dangerous.

IX

The philosophy of Spinoza is not perhaps a very good example. But reference to it is, I think, worthwhile. As we all know, Spinoza was condemned and rejected by the Synagogue. But he did not separate himself of his own accord from the Jewish faith. Nor was he concerned with denying the existence of God, as some of his hostile critics maintained. He was concerned with thinking the concept of God according to the criteria of what he believed to be rational philosophy. And in his opinion the concept of the Deity, when rendered intellectually viable, inevitably turned into the concept of *Deus seu Natura*, the infinite Substance of the *Ethica more geometrico demonstrata*. And though Spinoza talks about 'the intellectual love of God', he makes it clear that in his view anyone who desires that God should love him in return desires that 'the God whom he loves should not be God'.[19] If therefore we regard religion as involving a personal relationship between man and God, the encounter of faith, it is obvious that the transformation of the personal Deity of the Old Testament into *Deus seu Natura* excludes religion. For Spinoza's Substance is certainly not a personal being, not at any rate if the term 'personal' is used in anything approaching its ordinary range of meaning. Of course, if we understand religion as covering Spinoza's intellectual love of God and the whole process of liberation from the slavery of the passive emotions and elevation to the third degree of knowledge, Spinozism is certainly a religious philosophy. But we might wish to describe this religion as a philosophical substitute for orthodox Judaism.

It is true that Spinoza insisted on a radical distinction between faith and philosophy. Thus in the *Tractatus Theologico-politicus*[20] he asserts that faith (and theology) has as its aim the promotion of obedience and piety, whereas philosophy is concerned with truth. On this view a purely pragmatic value is attributed to biblical theology. A biblical doctrine may in fact be true; but it does not matter if it is not in fact true. For provided that it contributes to producing obedience and piety, truth has nothing to do with the matter. Even though therefore Spinoza has no wish to convert everyone to his philosophical religion and regards faith as suitable for most people, his account of faith is unlikely to satisfy the biblical theologian.

x

A particularly good example of what, for some theologians, constitute the worst features of metaphysics is provided by the philosophy of Hegel. In his mature thought at any rate Hegel came to think of himself as carrying on the programme of the medieval theologians, faith seeking understanding of itself. He represented himself as the champion of Christianity. And some of his warm admirers, such as J. H. Stirling, regarded him as being precisely this. After all, did not Hegel maintain that Christianity was the absolute religion, representing absolute truth? And whatever he may have said about Christianity in some of his early essays, did he not undertake to prove the truth of Christian dogmas? Was he not a great Christian apologist?

From the point of view of many theologians, however, the cloven hoof of metaphysics soon shows itself. Hegel tried, for instance, to exhibit in conceptual form the mystical insight of a writer such as Meister Eckhart into the relation between the finite spirit of man and the infinite divine Spirit. We can regard him as trying to develop a philosophical theism which would avoid the Scylla of conceiving God as a sort of additional being 'out there', over against the finite, and the Charybdis of identifying the One with the Many in such a way as to make the word 'God' a superfluous label for the world. The result of his efforts, however, was a concept of the divine reality which, in Kierkegaard's opinion, bore little resemblance to the God of the Christian religion. One would hardly pray to the Hegelian Absolute.

Again, though Hegel certainly maintained that Christian doctrines were true, he insisted that in the sphere of religion the truth is expressed in the form of pictorial thought, in the form adapted to the religious consciousness. Philosophy, however, thinks the same truth in purely conceptual form. Philosophy does not deny the doctrines of religion. On the contrary, it asserts and proves them. But this is done by substituting the form of logical sequence or necessity for the form of contingency. That is to say, truths expressed by religion in terms of historic events which, from the logical point of view, might or might not have occurred, are transformed by speculative philosophy into universal truths of reason. In a sense of course Hegel can be regarded as developing the form of apologetics which consists in trying to show the intrinsic truth of Christian doctrines without dependence on historic events.[21] But in the process of transformation into philosophical truths

Christian doctrines become something rather different from what they are for orthodox biblical theology.

Needless to say, the theologian is not committed to denying Hegel's contention that Christians use pictorial forms of thought. What he is likely to object to is the idea that it is for the metaphysical philosopher to decide what is the inner truth of a Christian belief. To say that we see through a glass darkly is one thing. To claim that the philosopher can see a good more clearly is something else.

In any case it seems to follow from Hegel's position that the truth of the Christian religion is made dependent on the truth of a particular philosophical system, namely absolute idealism. As McTaggart, himself an atheist, put it, Christianity becomes esoteric Hegelianism and Hegelianism esoteric Christianity. The Christian religion then stands or falls with absolute idealism. And the theologian can hardly be expected to welcome such a dependence of religious faith on a particular philosophy. This would apply of course in the case of philosophies other than that of Hegel. But Hegelianism provides, I suppose, the most impressive example of metaphysical philosophy substituting knowledge for faith and subordinating religion to itself.

XI

Now let us suppose that the theologian tries to interpret Christian experience and to state its implications. To put the matter linguistically, let us suppose that the Christian form of life finds its immediate experience in the language of worship and prayer. The theologian reflects on this first-order language. But in his reflections on its nature, presuppositions and implications he regards himself as committed to remaining faithful to the experience or form of life which expresses itself in the first-order language. When therefore he sees the metaphysician making nonsense of or at least downgrading the life of Christian worship and prayer by transforming the personal God into an impersonal Absolute to which nobody would think of praying and which could hardly be loved, he is likely to look on the metaphysician as an enemy. It is true of course that not all metaphysicians are devotees of the Absolute. But even in a, to him, more acceptable form of metaphysics the theologian may see the tendency to substitute the shaky conclusions of philosophical speculation for the faith which is born from encounter with the living God. This tendency is of course held in check when the philosopher is himself a devout Christian, as Bishop Berkeley was for instance. But even when metaphysics is used apologetically, to support faith, it is a support which faith can very well do without.

But is this attitude really satisfactory, however understandable it may be? Can the theologian in fact get along without metaphysics? And at what point is he going to halt the programme of faith seeking understanding of itself? Is metaphysics all right when it is a question of polytheistic Greeks and Hindus groping for the one God and all wrong when it is a question of philosophers at a later time seeking understanding of man and his world? This view may seem justified to the Christian theologian. But the philosopher is obviously likely to look at it in another light.

We can ask therefore whether there is perhaps some way of attributing a positive value to transcendent metaphysics even from the point of view of one who is committed to the belief that God has revealed himself in Christ. Or is a religious impulse simply misdirected when it finds expression in metaphysics? These are the questions we shall be dealing with in the next chapter.

3
Christian theology and metaphysics

THE term 'revelation' is often used in a vague sense, so that one does not know what precise meaning is being given to it. However, it is safe to say that all Christian bodies have traditionally believed that God revealed himself in a unique way in Christ, that Christ is Saviour in a unique sense, and that Christ pointed out to man the way of salvation. In other words, Christians in general have accepted the statement attributed to Christ that he is the way, the truth and the life[1] and the doctrine of St Paul that Christ is the unique mediator between God and man,[2] and that salvation is achieved through incorporation with Christ by the dwelling of the Holy Spirit.

Given this Christocentric outlook, it is easy to understand the hostility towards metaphysics which has been shown by a number of Christian theologians. For if metaphysics is regarded as taking the form of comprehensive world-views, with inbuilt ways of life, it inevitably tends to appear as a rival to Christian faith. According to Professor Zuurdeeg, for the metaphysician 'philosophy is both a saviour and a guide'.[3] And if we accept this statement we can hardly be surprised if a theologian welcomes modern criticism of metaphysics and the restriction of moral philosophy proper to an inquiry into the logic of ethical language. For it may seem to the theologian that in this way philosophy is put in its right place. It is disqualified from producing world-views and proclaiming ways of salvation. Philosophy becomes in a sense parasitic.[4] It can examine different language-games; but it is debarred from itself initiating a language-game in opposition to or as a rival to the Christian-language-game. It can examine other people's statements about the world and about human conduct. But it does not make statements of its own about reality in general or about the way in which human beings ought to behave. In a sense of course it can still trespass on the territory of the Christian theologian, but only by way of criticism, not by way of substituting other alleged truths for Christian truths, the truths of revelation.

Again, though a Christian theologian can accept the idea of development and even of restatement, he regards such development and restatement as relating to a Christian truth which does not become false overnight. It may indeed be difficult to combine successfully the idea of continuity and those of development and restatement. But the orthodox theologian presumably believes in some real sense in a permanent divine revelation to man. He is therefore likely to take a somewhat dim view of the succession of metaphysical systems, each of which is offered as the truth about reality. Metaphysics, as it is found in history, is likely to seem to him a sorry sort of business, promising much but achieving little.

A further point. If the theologian believes that Christ's mission is universal, that divine grace is offered to all, and that the leading of the Christian life does not depend on intellectual ability or philosophical acumen, is he likely to take a favourable view of any attempt to substitute for the gospel a metaphysical system, or a philosophical system of any kind? David Hume openly admitted that neither he nor anyone else could actually live by the scepticism which he entertained in his study. And though Kierkegaard looked on the philosophy of Hegel as a supreme intellectual *tour de force*, he stoutly maintained that it was not a philosophy by which man could live. Of course, a theologian might be prepared to allow that there could be a philosophical system by which some people at any rate could live. At the same time he would doubtless insist that in so far as a philosopher was inviting people to live by beliefs and standards which were incompatible with the Christian religion, he was misleading them. In fine, God has not chosen to save mankind by philosophy. And if philosophy sets itself up as a way of salvation, it is going beyond its proper limits. Modern criticism of metaphysics and the restriction of moral philosophy to discussion of the nature of ethical judgements and of ethical

D

languages have contributed to the desirable goal of confining philosophy within its proper bounds.

Now the general attitude which I have outlined is quite understandable. For it seems to me that there is a considerable difference between the respective relations to Christian theology of science on the one hand and of metaphysical systems on the other. It would indeed be rash to claim that there can be no tension between scientific *hypotheses* and traditional Christian beliefs. Obviously, if we adopt an interpretation of the Bible which does not involve our looking on it as a kind of scientific textbook, such clashes as that which gave rise to the Galileo affair can be ironed out. But even if a Christian is convinced that there can be no incompatability between established scientific truth and revealed truth, it would be extremely rash for him to deny the possibility of tension between scientific hypothesis or theory and a traditional Christian belief.[5] By and large, however, the so-called conflict between science and religion is a conflict not so much between science as such and religion as between a naturalistic world-outlook, fostered by the development of the particular sciences, and the supernaturalistic, traditional Christian vision of the world. Naturalism and positivism are philosophies rather than empirical science. And nobody doubts that a *philosophy* can be incompatible with Christianity. For a philosophy can occupy the same territory, so to speak, or part of it, as Christian belief, in a way in which natural science, by its very character, does not. And comprehensive metaphysical systems can appear as rivals to Christian theology in a way in which physics, for example, can hardly do. Natural science may appear to many people to render Christian belief superfluous or its truth improbable. But a metaphysical system can be directly incompatible with Christian belief in a way in which empirical science can hardly be. Natural science as such does not advance theories about 'ultimate reality'. Nor does it proclaim a way of salvation, a way to the blessed life. Philosophers, however, have sometimes done both these things. Hence there is no difficulty in understanding the hostility shown to metaphysics by a number of theologians who would not dream of attacking science as such.

Further, the theologian can doubtless point to the succession of metaphysical systems as evidence of the fruitlessness of metaphysics. Whitehead, when referring to the representation of European philosophical thought as 'littered with metaphysical systems, abandoned and unreconciled',[6] remarked that the history of science can also be represented as littered with abandoned hypotheses. And this is doubtless true. At the same time it would be absurd to deny that there has been an increase in scientific knowledge. It is obvious, for instance, that more is known now about nuclear energy than was known two hundred years ago. And it is obvious that chemical and medical knowledge is greater now than in the days of Paracelsus. No amount of talk about abandoned hypotheses can alter such obvious facts. It is not, however, obviously absurd to maintain that there has been no such advance in metaphysical knowledge. Some might argue that there has been. And others might argue that it is a great mistake to look for anything in metaphysics analogous to the accumulation of scientific knowledge, inasmuch as philosophy and empirical science are quite different pursuits. But my point is simply that while it would be obviously absurd for a theologian to deny that there has been an advance in scientific knowledge, it is not obviously absurd if he denies the cognitive value of metaphysical speculation. After all, on this point he would find himself in agreement with many people who have no use for theology, whereas he would certainly not find himself in agreement with them if he were so rash as to deny the advance in scientific knowledge.

It is certainly not my intention to commit myself to the view that metaphysics can have no cognitive value. I am merely concerned with pointing out both that a theological attack on metaphysics is quite understandable, from a theological point of view that is to say, and also that, in support of his attack, the theologian can appeal to lines of argument which carry weight even with critics of metaphysics who have little use for theology.

At the same time, even if a theological attack on metaphysics is understandable, I think that it is possible for the Christian theologian to combine a more positive appreciation of metaphysics with his understandable hostility to the claims advanced by some metaphysicians on behalf of their systems. And I now wish to explain what I have in mind.

II

Let us suppose that a man takes a swim in a river. If he looks round him, he sees the surface of the water, the banks, and other objects. What he sees is there to be seen. Otherwise he would not see it. But he cannot see the whole river. He might conceivably do so, if he went up in an aeroplane and the river were short enough. But immersed, as he is, in the stream he can see only a small part of it. And if he were to describe the whole river on the assumption that it must everywhere possess precisely the same characteristics as it has in the portion in which he is swimming, his description would doubtless be inaccurate. The volume of water will be smaller nearer the river's source, greater nearer its mouth. If the banks are low in the place where he is swimming, elsewhere the river may flow at the foot of high cliffs. At one point the river may be narrow and deep, at another point wide and shallow. And so on. At the same time the swimmer could make some true statements about the river as a whole, statements, that is to say, which must be true if it is proper to speak of a river at all. He could make such statements even though he had never seen the whole river.

To apply the analogy. The philosopher is necessarily in a definite historical situation. He is not an external spectator of the whole world or of all time and history. His vision and experience are necessarily limited. Nevertheless what he thinks that he sees may very well be there to be seen. The fact that his range of vision and experience is limited does not entail the conclusion that he is subject to hallucinations, or that what he claims to see is not objectively there to be seen. At the same time his attention may be so riveted on a particular aspect or feature of what he sees that he exaggerates its overall significance and transforms it, so to speak, into a key to unlock all doors. In other words, he makes it the determining basis of a comprehensive world-view. By acting in this way he may indeed draw attention in a forcible manner to something which may otherwise be neglected or minimised. His very exaggeration, or the one-sidedness of his interpretation of reality, may thus perform a useful function. But it remains an exaggeration, or a partial and distorted perspective.

An example may clarify the sort of idea I have in mind. When

Arthur Schopenhauer looked at the world and human life and history, he was struck by the evil and suffering which he found there. In fact suffering and pain seemed to him to be positive features of existence in a way in which happiness was not. He analysed happiness as being no more than a temporary cessation of pain. And he used the ideas of strife and suffering as a guide in determining the character of the ultimate reality which manifests itself in the world of phenomena.

In my opinion at least Schopenhauer's analysis of pleasure or happiness will not stand up to criticism. And whatever Buddhists may think about the matter, it seems to me that he exaggerated what we might describe as the dark side of the world and of human history, minimising other aspects. At the same time it is precisely Schopenhauer's exaggerations which draw forcible attention to very real aspects of the world and of human life, aspects which in some philosophies have been slurred over or explained away. His exaggeration, which was perhaps a needed complement or antithesis to some other philosophies, doubtless tended to evoke a reaction. But this does not alter the fact that, generally speaking, what Schopenhauer saw in the world was there to be seen. He threw into a clear light a very real aspect of the world and of human life, one that gives rise to standing problems in any theistic or pantheistic philosophy. It is doubtless possible to notice the evil and suffering in the world without indulging in Schopenhauerian metaphysics. But the fact that Schopenhauer drew metaphysical conclusions helps to show the urgency for religious belief of the problem of evil. For we can see his metaphysics as representing a possible way of seeing reality, if attention is focused on the phenomena of evil and suffering.

To avoid possible misunderstanding, I should explain that it is not my intention to suggest that mutually exclusive philosophical systems or world-views can be reconciled by the expedient of reducing each to a proposition which is obviously true. As they stand, the philosophies of Schopenhauer and Marx, for example, are mutually exclusive. If we reduced the philosophy of Schopenhauer to the statement that there is a large amount of evil and suffering in the world and the philosophy of Marx to the statement that unless man produces food and eats he cannot pursue scientific research or create works of art, the two statements would be true and compatible. But it would be absurd to pretend that by means of such a reduction one had reconciled the two philosophies. My point is rather that each philosophy gives expression to a genuine personal insight. In my opinion, however, in each philosophy an exaggerated significance is attached to a genuine insight in an overall inter- pretation of human life and history. An exaggeration of this kind can serve a useful purpose. But it remains an exaggeration. And the philosophy embodying it is a partial and one-sided vision.

Am I saying that there can be no such thing as a final and perennially true metaphysical system? My answer to this question is 'yes and no'. In other words, I should wish to make a distinction.

When using the analogy of a man swimming in a river, I emphasised the obvious fact that he cannot see the whole river, and that if he assumes that features of the portion of the river which he does see are characteristic of all sections of the river, the resulting description of the river as a whole is likely to be inaccurate. Obviously, I was referring to contingent features, features, that is to say, which do not belong necessarily to a river in the whole of its course. At the same time I admitted that the man could make true statements about the river as a whole, statements which must be true if it is legitimate to speak of a river at all. Analogously, if one means by a metaphysical system a world-view based on the assumption that some feature or features of the world, which could conceivably be absent or be otherwise than they are,[7] provide the key to the nature of reality as a whole, I do not think that there can be a final, adequate metaphysical system. For it remains possible to focus attention on other features and to construct a rather different world-view. At the same time I have no wish to deny that there can be propositions which must be true if we can speak of a world of finite things at all, and which express what might perhaps be described as the logical scaffolding of the world. In what precise sense such propositions can be exhibited as con- stituting a 'system' is open to discussion.[8] But if we are prepared to allow that a coherent arrangement of them could reasonably be described as a metaphysical system, I think that a perennially true metaphysical system is in principle possible.

It may be said that such propositions tend to express stale news, whereas world-views can be exciting and challenging, precisely because they constitute persuasive invitations to see the world in ways in which we do not necessarily see it. For example, let us assume that the statement that every finite thing is in principle capable of some form of change is perennially true, in the sense that if there is any finite thing, the statement must be true of it. Taken by itself at any rate this statement can hardly be considered exciting in the sense in which the statement that the phenomenal world is the self-manifestation of a blind 'will' is exciting, or the statement that the all-pervasive reality is the will to power, or the statement that all things are one. But the point at issue is whether there can be statements which are necessarily true if there is a world at all, not whether such statements constitute exciting news.

Now though every philosopher is necessarily located in a definite historical situation, he seeks conceptual mastery over reality as a whole. The drive to know the totality is there, even if the philosopher's knowledge is in effect limited. And in those philosophies in which the phenomenal world is looked on as ontologically dependent on an ultimate reality, on a One which is transcendent, at least in the sense that it cannot be simply identified with the world as it appears to us in sense-experience and in the sciences, this drive to conceptual mastery extends also to the One.[9] A philosopher can of course recognise limitations in this area. If, for example, he believes with St Thomas Aquinas in divine revelation of truths which transcend the reach of the human reason, he is likely to set limits to the scope of metaphysical knowledge. Again if he is a mystic, like Plotinus, he is likely to emphasise the ineffability of the God-head. But metaphysics when left to itself, so to speak, endeavours to capture all reality within the conceptual web of the human reason. Even if we adopt the view stated by Rudolf Carnap, that metaphysicians are poets or musicians who lack ability to write poetry or compose music and have chosen the wrong medium of expression, we have to add, with Carnap himself, that they have a strong theoretical urge, that 'they have a strong inclination to work with the medium of the theoretical, to connect concepts and thoughts'.[10] And this urge shows itself also in regard to the Transcendent, when, that is to say, the philosopher asserts or postulates the existence of the Trans-cendent. As has already been noted, it can be seen at work in, for example, the philosophy of Hegel, who attempted to trans-form the mystical insights of a Meister Eckhart into clear conceptual knowledge.

To utter a tautology, however, the Transcendent is the Transcendent. And that which is really transcendent pre-sumably transcends the conceptual web of the human reason. Obviously, some true statements can be made, namely those statements which must be true of any transcendent reality. For example, the Transcendent cannot be a member of the class of finite things, not at any rate if to say of a reality that it is trans-cendent means that it transcends this class. We can therefore use the word 'infinite', that is 'not-finite'. But the meta-physician, left to himself and impelled by his urge to know and to express his knowledge, is unlikely to be content with the 'negative theology' so dear to the heart of the mystics. On the contrary, he is likely to grasp at conceptual mastery and, in the process, to de-transcendentalise the Transcendent, if I may use such barbarous expressions. In this case, of course, one metaphysics of the Transcendent will evoke another. And in the end we shall have a succession of systems, each of which purports to reveal the nature of the ultimate reality.

Needless to say, some will see in this succession of systems of what Professor Walsh calls 'transcendent metaphysics' evidence in support of the conclusion that such philosophers are grasping at a phantom, which eludes their grasp precisely because it is a phantom. But I am concerned with the theologian and with his point of view. And what I am suggesting is that it is open to the theologian to see two things in the dialectic of systems of transcendent metaphysics. In the first place he can see in them, or at any rate in some of them, that genuinely religious impulse of which I spoke in the first chapter. In the second place he can see in the dialectic a witness to the divine trans-cendence and to the limitations of the human mind. He need not go so far as to claim that the metaphysician can make no true statements about God. For some statements must be true, if there is a Transcendent at all. But the theologian can insist that the metaphysician can hardly go beyond the scope of the so-called 'negative' theology, and that anything further must come, if it comes, through a divine self-revelation or self-manifestation. In other words, the theologian can, if he chooses, make an apologetic use of the succession of philosophical systems. He can see in transcendent metaphysics, whether oriental or western, an expression of the orientation of the human spirit to God. At the same time he can argue that the dialectic of systems bears witness to the fact that the veil over the Transcendent cannot be drawn aside simply by human effort and at will, but that it can be drawn aside only in so far as God discloses himself.

Obviously, if the theologian does adopt this sort of position, he is still faced by serious problems. For example, he may be challenged to show that Karl Jaspers was wrong in maintaining that the historical religions, including Christianity, no less than the historical systems of metaphysics, are so many 'decipherings' of the Transcendent, no one of which can be considered to possess final or universal validity. However, I am not concerned here with trying to solve the theologian's problems for him. I am simply concerned with pointing out a way in which he can attach a value to metaphysics, even though he sees in metaphysical systems an impulse to take by storm that which eludes the comprehension of the human mind. In other words, belief in revelation need not necessarily entail a complete rejection of metaphysics. For the theologian can see in metaphysics a movement of the human spirit towards God, while in the dialectic of systems he can see a historical self-limiting of the scope of speculative philosophy. Or he can see in the succession of systems the repeated raising of a question to which the answer can be given only through God's self-disclosure.

III

The metaphysical systems of which I have been talking are primarily of course the systems which have arisen since the medieval period—after, that is to say, philosophy had started to pursue a path of its own in separation from theology. In other words, I have envisaged the theologian as looking at philosophical systems from outside, as potential rivals. The question arises, however, whether the theologian should himself dispense with all metaphysics. And it is this question which I now wish to consider.

Perhaps I should emphasise the fact that I am not concerned with asking whether the Christian theologian is committed to adopting or taking under his wing, so to speak, a given historical system of philosophy. If he is going to make use of a philosophical system, there are obviously some limitations on his field of choice. If, for example, he believes in God and wishes to speak about God's saving activity, he can hardly adopt a philosophy which asserts that all talk about God is meaningless nonsense. If he does adopt such a philosophy, consistency seems to demand that he should then propose a radical change in Christian belief. But it is one thing to say that if consistency is to be respected, acceptance of traditional Christian belief excludes acceptance of philosophies which are incompatible with such belief; and it is another thing to maintain that there is only one particular philosophical system which a Christian theologian can adopt or utilise. And I have no wish to make this second claim. My question is rather whether the systematic theologian, if he is to do his job adequately, will find himself driven to what can reasonably be described as philosophical reflection.

It may appear that this is certainly not the case. For the Christian theologian as such, it may be said, faith is prior. Faith seeks understanding of itself; but faith comes first. And the process of faith seeking understanding gives birth to theology. If we attempt, for example, to articulate, systematise and develop the implications of the content of faith, we are doing theology, not philosophy. At no point is metaphysics required.

To put it another way, religious language can be described as the direct expression of religious attitudes or activities, such as prayer and worship. Or, more accurately perhaps, it is part of a religious act. As far as God is concerned, first-order religious language is talk *to* God rather than talk *about* God. It does not contain metaphysical assertions of God's existence but is addressed to the God of the Christian religious consciousness, the God of faith, the God revealed in Christ and encountered by Christians. Theology presupposes the first-order language of religion as a datum. It does indeed make statements about God.

But the God about whom it speaks is the God of the Bible, the God of Christian experience, and not the Absolute of the metaphysicians. Theological statements about God and his actions are not metaphysical conclusions but statements about the God of Christian faith. The theologian is an interpreter of God's word and of Christian experience. He is the vehicle, as it were, of the community's reflection on its own faith. He does not need metaphysics, and he can get along very well without it.

Indeed, it is arguable that the more metaphysical reflection is introduced into theology, the stronger becomes the tendency to develop an esoteric religion. Let us suppose, for example, that in order to find a meaning for the word 'personal' when predicated of the transcendent God the theologian tries to remove or cancel out the limitations of human personality. If he pursues this path of negation consistently, the positive content of the term is progressively eliminated. And the natural conclusion is that God is not a personal being—supra-personal no doubt, but not personal. The concept of God is thus transformed into that of the Absolute. We then get a division between the faith of simple-minded Christians and the higher knowledge of the metaphysically-minded, a division comparable to that between popular Hinduism and Hindu metaphysics. A kind of Gnosticism is developed which is foreign to the spirit of Christianity.

It may be objected that this is a gross exaggeration. For the type of theologian in question does not in fact deny that God is personal. He is concerned with ascertaining what it means to say that God is personal. It would be more accurate, however, to express the situation as follows. The natural conclusion at which the theologian in question should arrive is that God is not personal. But as a Christian he wishes to reach the conclusion that God *is* personal and thus to satisfy the demands of the Christian religious consciousness. He therefore creates, as F. H. Bradley puts it, 'a fog, where you can cry out that you are on both sides at once'.[11]

This state of affairs arises from the attempt to combine the language of Christian faith with that of metaphysics, when the two should be kept distinct. If the theologian is asked what he means by referring to God as personal, he should simply point to the ways in which the Bible represents God as acting. God issues commands; he hears prayers; he punishes the people of

Israel; he delivers them from their enemies; he reveals himself as a Father; he redeems mankind through Christ. In the Bible we find a God whose personal character is revealed through his actions in history. And reference to this self-revelation is quite sufficient to explain the use of the word 'personal'. The language of faith has its own internal rules. And the demand that it should conform itself to the language of metaphysics is as as unjustified as the demand that it should conform to the language of physical science.

IV

This sort of position can be expressed in a very persuasive manner. And it is easy to understand the fear that metaphysical reflection may transform Christianity into something else, or that it may foster the emergence of an esoteric religion, the religion of a few intellectuals. At the same time the position is open to criticism.

It is doubtless true, for example, that, as far as God is concerned, first-order religious language is talk addressed *to* God rather than talk *about* God.[12] However, the language of worship and prayer has ontological implications or makes ontological presuppositions. Provided that we are talking about sincere religious behaviour, it seems obvious to me that prayer to God presupposes that there is a God to whom prayer can sensibly be addressed. And it is not unreasonable to expect the theologian to make such presuppositions explicit and to reflect on the possibility of justifying them.

It is indeed open to the theologian to reply that if by justification we mean the process of supplying proofs of the existence of God, no such proofs can be given. Faith, he may claim, is a response to encounter with God, not assent to the conclusion of a philosophical proof. And if it is then asked how one can prove that alleged encounter with God *is* encounter with God, the reply can once more be made that no such proof can be given. The language of religious faith, it may be said, expresses a certain vision of reality and a certain total life-orientation. If this vision, this 'blik' (to use a term employed by Professor R. M. Hare) is presupposed, the believer sees things in a certain way. The Psalmist, for instance, sees in the world evidence of God's existence and action. But the evidence is evidence for the man of faith. Faith comes first. And the change from lack of faith to faith is a matter of conversion, not of argument. The validity of a 'blik' cannot be philosophically demonstrated; but there can be conversion from one 'blik' to another.

There is obviously some truth in this theory. If, for example, the Hebrew prophet sees the Bablyonian captivity as a divine punishment for his people's relapses into idolatry, he is not concerned with giving a rival account of the empirical events which would be mentioned by a secular historian. The empirical events are assumed; and the prophet is giving a religious interpretation of them. He sees them in the light of his faith and religious vision of history. His interpretation depends on and expresses his faith; and there is not question of proving its validity by what we might call 'neutral' philosophical arguments.[13]

To be sure, the question arises whether there is not some way of deciding between the claims of different 'bliks'. But it is arguable that any evidence whch may be offered to show that a given 'blik' is invalid or unreasonable counts as evidence only from the point of view of someone who has a different 'blik'. Consider Professor R. M. Hare's example of the student who firmly believes that the university dons are plotting his downfall or are conspiring to murder him.[14] The student is offered evidence to show that his belief is wrong. But the evidence offered is immediately interpreted by the student as evidence in favour of his belief. For instance, the friendly behaviour of a certain don is interpreted by the student as evidence of a subtle plot to allay his suspicions in preparation for a fell blow. Argument is useless. What is required is a cure. And, on the religious plane, it is conversion which corresponds to a cure. If it is objected that conversion is a cure only from the point of view of the man of faith, the retort can be made that the cure of the student is a cure only from the point of view of the majority which likes to regard its own 'blik' as sane and healthy.

The trouble with this point of view is that to give a theoretical justification of it we have to appeal to the same logical criteria which are appealed to by those who wish to attack it. The The student may misuse logic, but he uses it. How, he asks, can you possibly know that the conduct of the friendly seeming don is to be taken at its face value? We may not accept this argument; but it is an argument. It seems to me therefore that we can reasonably cast doubt on the validity of a certain 'blik' by argument. We can point out, for example, that it is incompatible with another belief which is firmly held by the man in question, and that he therefore ought to abandon one or the other. We could argue in this way, if a man held, for example, that science provides us with knowledge and at the same time held a belief which was incompatible with the first belief. Or we can argue that while a view of things proposed by someone is compatible with his other beliefs and cannot be proved to be wrong, there is nothing which would normally count as a positive reason for thinking it true. Obviously, if a man simply rejects all logical thought, we cannot argue with him. But if he accepts logical criteria, argument is possible.

It is not my intention simply to reject the 'blik' idea. If a man is asked why he interprets a certain set of events in a certain way and he explains that the interpretation is governed by a certain overall vision of history, we have a better understanding of the situation, especially of course if we see that his interpretation is in fact authorised, even if not entailed, by his overall vision or 'blik'. At the same time it is difficult to see why it should be illegitimate to ask the man whether in his opinion adoption of this overall vision or 'blik' is simply a matter of choice or whether he can offer reasons for adopting it. To be sure, one cannot expect everyone to be in a position to cite evidence in support of his or her 'blik'. But it hardly seems unfair if one invites the theologian to say whether he thinks that reasons can be given for adopting the vision, and so the language, of faith, and, if so what these reasons are.

Let me express the matter in another way. It is easy to jump on the Wittgensteinian band-wagon, so to speak, and to claim that if a certain language-game is actually played, no further justification is required. In this case, I suppose, the empirical fact that a certain language-game has fallen, or appears to be falling, into disuse constitutes by itself an adequate reason for discarding it. But is this the case? I do not think that those who maintain that talk about God should be discarded are simply registering the empirical fact that disbelief in God is widespread. They are presumably convinced that there is no good reason for supposing that there is a God to talk about. And those who think that talk about God should not be discarded are presumably convinced that there *is* a God to talk about. Hence the theologian who is professionally concerned with the language of faith, can be invited without impropriety to say whether in his opinion any justification can be given of the use of this language.

The theologian may reply that there can be only an internal justification. This seems equivalent to a repetition of the claim that language-games are autonomous and self-justifying. But consider for a moment the Christian thinkers who reinterpret Christianity in such a way as to eliminate belief in a transcendent God. They would hardly undertake such a radical transformation of the Christian religion, unless they had accepted, at least implicitly, a theory of being from which it followed that talk about a transcendent God was meaningless nonsense.[15] In other words their interpretation is governed by a presupposed theory of being or metaphysics. Similarly, if it is maintained that statements about a transcendent God can be genuine, meaningful assertions, this position seems to me to presuppose an at any rate implicit theory of being or metaphysics. And it can legitimately be expected of an adequate theology that it should make explicit its own presuppositions.

v

As I have referred to the theory of autonomous and self-justifying language-games, I wish to clarify somewhat my position. In what I have been saying hitherto I have used the term language-games to refer to scientific discourse, religious discourse, ethical discourse, and so on. And I have no intention of calling in question Wittgenstein's statement that if we wish to ascetain the meaning of a term or proposition, we should examine its use in the context of the language-game in which it has its native home.[16] To treat a theological proposition, such as 'God loves all men' as though it were a hypothesis of physical science would be absurd. At the same time the term 'language-games' can be used to refer to such activities as asserting, questioning, commanding, exclaiming, and so on. A language-game in this sense, such as asserting, may be found both in scientific discourse and in religious discourse. In this case the question arises whether there are not certain basic and common requirements for a genuine assertion, whether it belongs to scientific or to religious discourse. For example, must not a genuine assertion assert something? And can it assert something without excluding something, namely its contradictory?

The point of these remarks is that if the theologian is asked for the meaning of a theological assertion, it is not sufficient to reply that it belongs to the language of Christian faith and must be understood in this context. The reply is true enough; but it is not sufficient if, that is to say, an assertion, to be a genuine assertion, must satisfy some basic requirements of intelligible discourse which are not confined to the language of faith. And in this case the autonomy of the religious language-game is limited.

Needless to say, I am not engaged in making the covert suggestion that theological assertions cannot pass the test. For example, it seems clear to me that the statement that God loves all men as a Father excludes the statement that he created men in order to assign them all to eternal torment. In my opinion the two statements are incompatible. And if this is correct, the theologian can meet the objection that the statement that God loves all men asserts nothing because it excludes nothing. It may not exclude the statement that there will be wars. But when seen in the context of the language-game in which it has its native home, it does exclude something, and though in showing that this is the case the theologian may refer throughout to the language of faith, he is none the less showing that a theological statement fulfils a requirement relating to all factual assertions.

It may be said that I have shifted my ground. I set out to question the thesis that the theologan can get along perfectly well without metaphysics; but I am now talking about semantic questions or matters of logical or linguistic analysis. But suppose that a theologian is asked what it means to say that God created the heavens and the earth or, more simply, the world. It is difficult to see how he can explain the meaning of the statement without saying something that can fairly be described as metaphysical talk. Or suppose that a theologian says that God's existence cannot be proved, inasmuch as God is transcendent; and that to assert the probability of God's existence is implicity to deny the divine transcendence. It may appear that he is rejecting metaphysics. And he is indeed rejecting a particular metaphysical position or claim. But how can he throw light on the meaning of the term 'transcendent' without making metaphysical remarks?

VI

In this chapter I have referred frequently to 'the theologian'. It is scarcely necessary to explain that I have not envisaged one man fulfilling all the tasks to which I have alluded. I am not, I hope, so foolish as to reject or belittle specialisation. For that matter, I have not necessarily understood the word 'theologian' in the sense in which the Christian theologian would be distinguished from the Christian philosopher. I have had in mind the Christian thinker, whether he would classify himself as a theologian or a philosopher, for whom faith constitutes the point of departure. And my general contention has been that the process of faith seeking understanding of itself must lead at some point or other to what can reasonably be described as metaphysical reflection. I do not mean that faith must be changed into something else, nor that it must give birth to an autonomous metaphysical system which serves as a new or esoteric religion. I have been talking throughout of the process of *fides quaerens intellectum*, of the displaying of a total Christian vision and of working out its presuppositions and implications.

In a real sense therefore I have been defending the process which led from the original preaching of the gospel to the medieval theological-philosophical syntheses, a process which some seem to regard as unfortunate and a mistake. I hasten to add, however, that I am not concerned with defending medieval thought as such, as though it were definitive and final. On the contrary, I am convinced that later ages require fresh efforts. But I am equally convinced that an adequate understanding of the Christian faith requires philosophical reflection, and that it is not facilitated by a wholesale rejection of metaphysics.

E

4
Modern philosophy and religion

In the last chapter reference was made to problems of meaning in regard to talk about God. In the first part of the present chapter I wish to take up this theme again. As recent philosophy of religion in this country and in the United States has been largely devoted to reflection on religious language, no apology is needed for dealing with this subject.

It is probably true to say that most people who have been brought up in a definite historic religion in which the concept of God plays a central role fail to see anything odd or peculiar, as far as meaning is concerned, in the statements about God to which they are accustomed. They may come to doubt the *truth* of such statements. To take an obvious example, advertence to the sufferings of children, the incurable diseases of loved ones, world-devastating wars, the cruelty of man to man, and so on may lead people to doubt whether it is true to say that there is an all-knowing and all-powerful God who loves all men as a Father. But it does not normally occur to Christians to doubt whether this statement is meaningful. The ordinary Christian understands the statement that God loves us in a quite straight-forward way. He is perfectly well aware of course that the statement that God loves us as a Father is not intended to imply that God is one's Father in precisely the same sense as one's earthly father. But he does not understand the term 'love' in some Pickwickian sense. Nor, ordinarily speaking, does any semantic problem occur to him in this respect.

If, however, one did raise and press problems of this kind, the ordinary Christian would doubtless feel that his religion was being threatened. If he comes across metaphysical or theological talk about divine transcendence or immanence or something of the sort, he is likely to feel that this is technical language which

54

is employed by academics but which has little bearing on his religious life. In the case of the concept of God as a loving Father, however, the situation is different. For this analogy governs his attitude to God and to other people. Or at any rate he believes that it should do so. If therefore the meaningfulness of the analogy is called in question, he naturally feels that it is not simply a case of esoteric discussion between theologians or metaphysicians, but that his religion is under fire.

It is of course an obvious fact that some philosophers have pressed semantic problems in regard to religious language in a polemical and destructive spirit. We can all think of books which are clearly directed to the undermining of at any rate theocentric religion. And the ordinary Christian might very well see in such books confirmation of his belief that reflection on problems of meaning is a threat to religion. Here, however, I wish to suggest another point of view, even if I approach it in what may appear to be a rather roundabout manner.

II

Reflection on religious language is not simply a modern phenomenon. In the thirteenth century, for example, St Thomas Aquinas discussed problems of meaning in regard to statements about God and developed a theory of analogical predication, a topic which was taken up by leading Thomists such as Cajetan and John of St Thomas. It is doubtless true that in the main streams of modern philosophy the subject was comparatively neglected. However, Berkeley made some remarks on the topic.[1] So did Kant.[2] And Hegel expounded a theory of the thinking and language appropriate to the expression of the religious consciousness. It may be true, or rather it is true, that it is only in modern times that the sort of theme discussed by Aquinas in the Middle Ages has become the subject of widespread discussion; but the theme itself is not a novelty.

At the same time modern discussion of religious languages cannot be properly represented as no more than the resumption of a medieval discussion. For there are obvious differences. For one thing, though Aquinas made some general remarks about language, he was chiefly concerned with talk about God, whereas contemporary discussions of religious language form part of a more general inquiry into the different types and functions of language. For another thing, whereas Aquinas' attention was focused principally on assertions about the nature of God, emphasis is often laid today on the complexity of religious language, not only in regard to the different types of religious utterances but also in regard to the variety of functions which may be performed by given utterances.[3] Obviously, there is no good reason to suppose that Aquinas, were he alive today, would hesitate to recognise the legitimacy of this broadening of the scope of the discussion. But there has in fact been such a broadening. Further, whereas Aquinas' discussion was carried on within the area of Christian theology, today it is carried on by believers and unbelievers alike.

Though, however, there are differences in context and in the scope of the discussion as carried on in the Middle Ages and in the modern world, in both cases the emphasis is placed principally on talk about God. And this is only to be expected. For if we attempt to talk about a God who is *ex hypothesi* transcendent and infinite, problems of meaning are bound to arise, which do not arise if we are engaged in talking about Zoroaster or the prophet of Islam. Further, to all intents and purposes religion in the West has meant for centuries principally Christianity or, more generally, the Judaeo-Christian tradition. And Judaism and Christianity are both theocentric religions, even if original Buddhism is not. Hence it is in no way surprising if in western philosophy, discussion of religious language tends to concentrate on talk about God, today as in the Middle Ages.

Even if we keep to this sphere, however, we can see an important difference between the medieval approach and that adopted by some contemporary authors. If we look at the writings of Aquinas, we find him treating first of the existence of God considered, for example, as first (supreme) and uncaused cause or as the absolutely necessary being, and only afterwards of the analogical use of terms in statements about the divine nature and activity. Needless to say, his own personal assurance of the existence of God comes from faith rather than from metaphysical argumentation. And he naturally assumes that the statements made about God in orthodox Christianity must be meaningful, even though he sees that there are problems of meaning in regard to them. But even if to some extent Aquinas is following a traditional pattern of treatment, we can say, I think, that for him the existence of a subject of predication is the logically prior theme. Thus he would doubtless say that before we can profitably reflect on talk about God, we had better assure ourselves that there is something to talk about. If, however, we look at the writings of some modern authors, we find them insisting that the problem of meaning is prior to the question of existence. That is to say, before we can profitably inquire whether there is sufficient evidence for asserting the existence of God, we must first assure ourselves that the concept of God is free from internal self-contradiction and incoherence. For if the concept turns out to be a self-contradictory or a thoroughly incoherent idea, it is waste of time to ask whether there is a God. 'This question of consistency' is 'logically prior to that of existence.'[4]

III

Now it seems obvious to me that those who insist on the priority of the question of meaning or, as Flew puts it, of consistency can make out a strong case for their position. It is true that they sometimes use unfortunate expressions which imply that the concept of God is the concept of a member of a class with a plurality of members, so that it makes sense to talk about 'picking out' God, as one might try to pick out a specimen of a certain kind of animal, bird, insect or plant in a Brazilian forest. Similarily, talk about asking whether there is a God who instantiates the idea of God may be taken to imply that 'God' is a universal concept of which there could in principle be more than one instantiation.[5] But it is not necessary that those who insist on the priority of the problem of meaning should use such ways of speaking. It is sufficent for them to maintain that before we can profitably discuss the existence of God, we must first assure ourselves that the concept of God is not self-contradictory and that the existence of God is thus a possibility, and this is far from being an unreasonable point of view. Jean-Paul Sartre has maintained that the idea of God is in fact self-contradictory. And if we accepted his thesis, would we really think it worth our while to inquire into the existence of God? Not, it may be said, unless we adopt a rather different attitude to logic from that which generally prevails in the West.[6]

At the same time the notion of first establishing the logical possibility of God and then looking round to see whether there is any evidence for there actually being a God is likely to strike a good many religious people as artificial and repugnant. The reason for this, it may be said, is that they have been brought up to believe in God and are not prepared to suspend their belief while talk about God is submitted to critical analysis. But this seems to me a superficial account of the matter. In my opinion real belief in God, as distinct from mere repetition of formulas of belief, is a response to a divine self-manifestation, not indeed as an intuited object, but as the attracting goal of a movement or as a mysterious presence, 'within' as well as 'without'. I thus find myself in agreement with a recent writer when he asserts the possibility of 'the sense of God's reality'.[7] It can occur, as the writer says, in different contexts; and it can take different forms. But occur it does. And if we recognise that real belief in God expresses a sense of God's reality, it is easy to understand why it is possible for a religious person to recognise the difficulties and problems which arise in connection with talk about God and yet be convinced that, however peculiar in some respects the language may be, it is about something—that there is, in other words, a subject of predication. Indeed, it is possible for a man to come to the conclusion that talk about God is an attempt to say what cannot be said and that silence would be the best policy, and yet remain firmly convinced that in talking about God we are trying, even if unsuccessfully, to talk about a reality. To such a man there is an element of absurdity in the notion that all belief in a divine reality should be suspended until the idea of God has been tidied up to the satisfaction of a logical analyst and until sufficient evidence for God's existence has been produced to satisfy the empiricist.

Of course, it may be objected that I am introducing psychological considerations, which are irrelevant to a purely logical issue. Let us assume that real belief in God does rest on some sort of experience. To describe this psychological event as an experience of God, of a divine reality, is to give an interpretation. And before such an interpretation can be considered legitimate, it has to be shown that the concept of God is free from internal contradictions. For if the concept of God is a self-contradictory idea, we cannot be justified in describing any experience as an experience of God. The same holds good, even if the term 'God' is understood in a minimal sense, as meaning, for instance, ultimate reality or ground of finite existence, without further determination. For if the notion of, say, ground of finite existence is incoherent, we cannot be justified in claiming that any experience is an experience of the ground of finite existence. Such a claim may very well be psychologically understandable. But it does not follow that it is justifiable from a logical point of view.

This is a persuasive line of argument. It is arguable however that it involves a questionable presupposition, namely that a language can be adequately understood by looking at it in abstraction from the function or functions which it performs. It is hard, to suppose, for example, that ethical language can be adequately understood by inspecting terms such as 'right', 'wrong', 'good', 'bad' and 'ought' in abstraction. Of course nobody in his senses would think that such ethical terms can be understood without considering their uses or functions within ethical language, an activity which involves reflection on examples of use. But my point is that ethical language as a whole, the ethical language-game, cannot be adequately understood without consideration of the role which it plays in human life. Indeed, consideration of man himself as a social being is required. On this subject Professor Stuart Hampshire has remarked that 'the different uses of language have ultimately to be understood as acts of communication, and therefore as parts of different forms of social life . . . Philosophy as linguistic analysis is therefore unwillingly lured into a kind of descriptive anthropology.'[8] In regard to religious language, this again cannot be adequately understood apart from consideration of its functions. And if talk about God is basically a way of referring to and speaking of what a man regards as that which discloses itself in certain types of experience, we cannot adequately understand the language apart from the basic experience or types of experience.

As religious language, including talk about God, is already in existence and has been in existence for many centuries, and as at the same time there are many people who deny that or doubt whether the term 'God' has objective reference, the claim that the problem of meaning is logically prior to the problem of

existence is certainly understandable. And if a man starts talking about an intuitive awareness of God or a sense of God's
reality or something of the sort, it is perhaps natural to think of
him as grasping at a ready-made instrument in order to
describe or refer to a psychological experience which may be a
purely subjective occurrence. But if we think in this way, we
neglect the possibility that the instrument—that is, the language, has grown up and been developed in response to a need
of referring to the experience in question, and that this connection may be important in determining features of the
language. For example, if the experience is *sui generis* or unique,
we cannot exclude the possibility that this fact helps to explain
odd or peculiar features of the language. After all, if there is in
some sense an experience of a hidden or mysterious ultimate
reality, we would hardly expect that it could be adequately
referred to in language which has been developed in response
to the need of being able to talk about finite things in the world.
If such language is used, it is bound to undergo strains and
stresses in the process.

Needless to say, I am perfectly well aware that these sketchy
remarks do not solve all relevant problems. If we wish to speak,
for example, of an intuitive awareness of God, we are faced with
a number of questions, both theological and philosophical. We
can hardly postulate an intuition of God himself, in a sense
which would involve attributing to believers what theologians
have called the beatific vision. Apart from the extravagance of
such a claim, it would then be very difficult to allow for faith or
to account for states of mind which do not amount to unbelief
but which certainly do not exemplify any clear intuition of God
himself. Again, even if it is claimed that the basis awareness of
God is *sui generis*, we still have to explore possible analogies
to it in other contexts, at any rate if we wish to discuss it. But
though to draw attention to such questions is to confirm what I
maintained in the last chapter, namely that an adequate
theology will involve reflection which can be fairly described as
philosophical, I cannot undertake to discuss these questions
here. I must content myself with repeating that in my opinion
it is a mistake to suppose that we can have an adequate understanding of religious language in general, and of talk about
God is particular, without reflection on the reason or reasons

why this language-game is played. If we wish to understand this language, we are driven to reflect on man and his experience. We can then understand better certain features of the language. We can also understand why some people remain convinced that in spite of any pecularities or oddities which may be detectable in it, talk about God is talk about something; that if all the oddities were ironed out, talk about God would no longer be talk about *God*; and that if antecedent belief in a subject of predication is cancelled out, so to speak, inquiry into talk about God becomes a purely academic discussion of a dead language.

IV

So far I have simply assumed that there are problems of meaning in regard to talk about God. I shall now offer one or two examples. But as the subject is probably familiar to us all, I do not intend to discuss the matter at length.

My first example is by no means a novel one. We are often told by theologians, that God is not 'a being', a member of a class with a plurality of members, an object among objects or thing among things. Well and good. I have no wish to quarrel with such statements. At the same time it seems that unless we propose to use the word 'God' as a superfluous label for the world, we cannot refer to God or speak about him without distinguishing him from all finite things. In this case, however, how can we avoid speaking of him as 'a being'? We can of course describe God as infinite. But must not the infinite comprise all reality? If God is distinguished ontologically from finite things, does not the word 'infinite', as applied to God, become an honorific title, signifying the greatest member of a class? In brief, the transcendent and infinite God cannot be a member of a class with a plurality of members. But it appears that we cannot think of him at all without implying that this is precisely what he is. Theistic talk thus seems to be incoherent. Matters are not indeed improved by embracing pantheism. For if finite things are said to be parts of God, what can this possibly mean? And if God is identified with the world, the word 'God', as I have already suggested, seems to be a superfluous label. But the shortcomings of pantheism, it may be said, do not rescue theism from the charge of incoherence.

Philosophers and theologians have of course endeavoured to cope with this problem. Some have abandoned the claim that God is infinite and have adopted the theory of a finite Deity. It can then be admitted quite frankly that God is what our language implies that he is, namely a being, though the greatest of them. But though some people may, and doubtless do, find solace in the idea of God as a finite and limited fellow-struggler who needs their help, the result, it seems to me, of the reduction of God to a being within the universe is simply that the religious mind soon goes beyond 'God' to *God*, passing beyond the human all-too-human picture of God to Tillich's unconditioned Transcendent. And then we are back again where we were before. God is not 'a being'. But how can we refer to or speak of him without implying that this is precisely what he is?

The Thomists have had recourse to the theory of the analogy of being. God is infinite being. And as finite beings are not being in the same univocal sense, we cannot add the finite to the infinite to make a sum-total greater than the infinite. As the Scholastic dictum puts it, creation involves more beings but not more being.

This may very well be the sort of thing which we have to say if we wish to claim at one and the same time that God is infinite and that finite things are ontologically distinct from him. That is to say, in order to show that these two statements are compatible it may very well be the case that we have to embrace a theory of the analogy of being. True, Karl Barth, if I am not mistaken, was hostile to the theory. But it is very difficult for me to see how, without such a theory, we could talk meaningfully about God at all. At the same time, though I am perfectly prepared to admit that traditional theism demands a theory of analogy, I cannot claim that statements such as 'creation involves more beings but not more being' are crystal clear to me.

It may be said that this sort of talk is metaphysics. If we avoid it and keep to the language of the Bible, such conundrums do not arise. Well, this may be true at a certain level. In the Bible, talk about God is generally directed to evoking responses in attitude and conduct: it is not speculative philosophy. For example, God is represented as willing this or commanding that. And a command is obviously intended to secure obedience. But I have already raised the question in a previous chapter whether we are prepared to adopt the thesis of Spinoza that the language of faith, the language of the Bible, is not concerned with truth. If we are not prepared to adopt this thesis, I do not see how we can justifiably prohibit reflection on the presuppositions and implications of biblical utterances. For instance, the representation of God as issuing commands clearly implies that God is personal. An impersonal Absolute does not issue commands. What, however, does it mean to speak of God as personal? That he is intelligent, for example? What does *this* mean? Well, there are doubtless some things that it cannot mean. But to say what the term does not mean is not quite the same thing as to say what it does mean.

Aquinas remarked that 'we cannot understand of God what he is, but (only) what he is not and how other things are related to him'.[9] But do we in fact understand how finite things are related to God? We say, for example, that all finite things depend on him as creatures in relation to their Creator. Apart, however, from difficulties arising out of the idea of creation itself, it is none too easy to specify the notion of dependence in this context. The notion can of course be delimited, in the sense that the theologian or philosopher can say what it is not. For instance, a finite thing's relation of dependence on God can hardly be identical with its relations of dependence on other finite things. If it were, then to say that all finite things depend on God would not add anything to saying that they depend in a variety of ways on one another. Nor can the relation of dependence on God be of the same order as, though additional to, empirical relations of dependence. If it were, a finite thing would presumably depend partly on God and partly on other finite things, whereas the theologian wishes to say that a finite thing depends wholly on God. Of course, if the relationship is unique, as presumably it is, it cannot be adequately explained in terms of other kinds of relationship. But this fact does not provide us with a clear insight into the nature of the relationship to God. I do not mean that nothing can be said to facilitate understanding; but that all things depend on God is something which, given certain premises, we have to say, rather than something the meaning of which is plain to our minds.

From one point of view of course this does not matter. The statement that all finite things depend on God can perfectly well mean something to a man in the sense that it can influence his life and conduct. That is to say, he can live in the light of the conviction that he himself and everything else depend on God. But if we look on the statement that all things depend on God as true in a sense which would satisfy the correspondence theory of truth, we can hardly deny the fact that logical analysis can raise some pretty difficult questions.

Given this situation, one can understand a man suggesting that talk about God is an attempt to say what cannot be said and that the best policy would be one of silence. Though, however, this policy may be attractive to the mystically-minded (chatter about God is disagreeable to many people in any case), there are at any rate two reasons against it. The first is practical or pragmatic. Christianity, Judaism and Islam are social religions. Christianity, for example, regards itself as having a universal mission and recognises the call to spread the gospel. And as this can hardly be done without speech, talk about God is unavoidable, unless perhaps we propose to undertake a radical revision of the Christian religion and eliminate the concept of God. The second reason is more theoretical. It is indeed possible to abstain from speech, from the use of what Ockham called the *verbum prolatum*. It would be *possible* not to mention God, even in sermons. We could suppress all public prayers addressed to God. But if we propose to pray interiorly to God or to worship him or to strive after union with him or to think of him in any way, we necessarily form a concept of God which is in principle communicable. In other words, we cannot avoid *interior* speech, which *could* be vocalised. Hence it is questionable whether a complete and consistently maintained policy of silence is possible, except at the cost of eliminating even the thought of God. I have no wish to dogmatise about the relation between thought and language. I am not prepared to state categorically that there cannot be thought without language, wordless thought. But my view, for what it is worth, is that thought and language stand to one another in a relation which can perhaps be best described in terms of Aristotle's theory of 'form' and 'matter'. And I doubt at any rate whether it is possible to retain belief in God and at the same time observe a policy of total and complete silence, unless indeed by silence we mean simply abstention from external speech.

Now if belief in God involves the use of language, even if not of externalised speech, we need rules for the use of concepts or terms.[10] Even if we invented an entirely new language in order to refer to and talk about God, we should still need rules. Such rules, it seems to me, can be of various kinds. In the relevant context metaphysical language seems to be determined, in large part at least, by rules for the exclusion of certain predicates. For example, if there is an ultimate reality which transcends the class of finite things, we must exclude the predicate 'finite'. We must therefore speak of the ultimate reality as not-finite, that is as infinite. A definite historical religion, however, can have its own rules. For example, for the Christian, use of the analogy of a Father in thinking and speaking of God is warranted by the authority of Christ. It is part and parcel, so to speak, of the Christian language-game. And understanding and use of the analogy are determined in the long run by the Christian community itself. Of course, apart from the fact that different Christian bodies have somewhat different conceptions of the nature and role of authority in this sphere, in practice it is largely the theologians who interpret the experience of the Christian community and its understanding of divine revelation. But whatever roles we may attribute to ecclesiastical authority or to theologians or to written documents, all these, when considered as providing rules for the use of language, are internal to the Christian community, not external to it.

Provided that we have certain rules for the use of terms in talk about God, I doubt whether the semantic problems which arise are quite so important, from a religious point of view, as some people seem to think. For example, in the New Testament we are told that 'God is love'.[11] Again, Christ is recorded as having said 'I am the truth'.[12] A logical analyst, if he so chooses, can make fun of both statements. In any case he can raise difficulties in regard to their meaning. But from the religious point of view it is clearly irrelevant to remark, for instance, that love is an abstract noun or that Christ can hardly be identified with truth if truth is defined in terms of a philosophical theory of truth, such as the correspondence theory or the instrumentalist theory. From the religious point of view the important thing is to love other human beings as children of God (which is precisely, the lesson which St John is ramming home) or to look to Christ as teacher of the way of salvation.

Once, however, we reflect critically on talk about God, the sort of problems or questions to which I have alluded certainly arise. As has already been noted, simple-minded Christians may tend to regard the raising of such questions as equivalent to an attack on their faith or to a subtle undermining of it. Indeed, even more sophisticated Christians may feel in much the same way. But if God is transcendent, he must presumably transcend the reach of what we are able to comprehend in thought and adequately express in language. To be sure, we need consistent rules of speech. The divine transcendence does not mean that we can say anything which takes our fancy. But our statements will need qualification, the qualification being by way of explanation.[13] But adequate conceptual representation and linguistic expression of the transcendent and infinite are impossible and are not to be expected. And recognition of the fact that in being used to refer to and speak of God our language undergoes strains and stresses can serve to remind us that it is *God* of whom we are speaking, a God whom we can represent with the aid of analogies but who cannot be taken by storm and imprisoned within the web of our concepts.

Spinoza declared that he had as clear and distinct an idea of the divine essence as he had of the essence of a triangle.[14] It seems to me that St Thomas Aquinas was nearer the mark when he said that 'he knows God best who acknowledges that whatever he thinks and says falls short of what God really is'.[15] If Aquinas were alive today, he would doubtless try to exhibit the internal logic of religious language; but he would hardly be dismayed at its failure to make God plain to view. Nor of course would a mystic such as St John of the Cross. To take but one example, St John of the Cross asserts that God falls within no genus or species and then remarks that 'the soul in this life is not capable of receiving in a clear and distinct manner aught save that which falls into a genus and a species'.[16] If therefore St John of the Cross were told that while God is said not to be a member of a class with a plurality of members, our talk about God suggests that this is what he is, he would not be surprised. His comment might very well be that if we once recognise the shortcomings of our language in this context, we have taken a step forward in understanding the implication of such statements as that God is 'incomparable, incomprehensible and so forth'.[17] To put the matter bluntly, the mystic might well maintain that while critical analysis of talk about God can obviously be pursued in an anti-religious spirit, it can also help us to surmount a certain species of idolatry and come to have a more fitting idea of God.

v

Now I can imagine the following sort of reaction to what I have been saying. 'There is no need at all to make such a song and dance about inquiry into the logic of religious language. Considered in itself, it is no more a threat to religion than inquiry into the logic of ethical language is a threat to morality, or reflection on scientific language a threat to science. There are indeed some people who think that talk about God is riddled with inconsistencies and incoherence. But if they press this point of view in a polemical spirit, it is probably because they think that belief in God is prejudicial to man's intellectual and moral development. There are surely many more people who simply find talk about God irrelevant. They may be perfectly prepared to agree with you that in talk about a transcendent God language is bound to undergo strains and stresses. After all, this is pretty obvious. But it is precisely talk about a transcendent God which they find irrelevant.

'You have tried to find a link between the puzzles which arise when one reflects on talk about God and the mystic's dissatisfaction with talk *about* God. Fair enough. The religious mystic feels the need of God: he seeks for union with the Godhead. For him therefore the idea of God is clearly relevant. Further, the religious mystic has always felt that the divine reality with which he seeks union cannot be adequately expressed in language. Even Richard Jefferies, who regarded himself as an atheist and is generally described as a nature mystic, said that he was looking for "something higher than soul—higher, better, and more perfect than deity".[18]

'Again the idea of God is clearly relevant in the eyes of those who, even if they are not mystics, feel that they cannot achieve salvation or lead the sort of life which they consider desirable without supernatural aid. But most people are not mystics. And some at least look on mysticism as a form of escapism, a sterile turning-away from urgent tasks and duties in the world. Again, there is an increasing number of people who think that man can quite well lead a moral life and strive after the realisation of ideal values without the help of any supernatural power. To such people talk about God is simply irrelevant. Discussion of its logical characteristics does not interest them except perhaps as confirmation of its irrelevance.

'Surely therefore the theistic philosopher would be more profitably engaged in trying to show the relevance of talk about God than in discussing possible relations between logical analysis and mysticism. It may be said that this is not the philosopher's business. He can indeed point out that the question whether talk about God is relevant invites further questions such as "Relevant for whom?" or "Relevant in what respect?" And he can give examples of cases in which the idea of God appears relevant and examples of cases in which it does not. But it is not the job of a philosopher to persuade people who find the idea of God irrelevant that it is in fact relevant or that they ought to find it relevant. Though, however, this attitude fits in well with one conception of the philosopher's role, this conception is one which makes a good many people extremely impatient. They expect the philosopher to concern himself with what is relevant to man and society and not to devote himself to the playing of academic games.

'The philosopher may of course reply that it is not his business to usurp the role of moralist or preacher or political saviour. But in adopting this attitude he is letting himself off too lightly. Even if we do not accept a pragmatist or instrumentalist definition of truth, we cannot dismiss out of hand William James' contention that if two beliefs or theories have exactly the same "consequences", it is a matter of indifference which belief or theory we embrace. Any philosopher who asserts the existence of God must be prepared to meet this claim. He ought to endeavour to show that belief in God makes a difference, and so that it is relevant.'

VI

t seems to me that there is a good deal of truth in this line of

thought. But it is intellectual relevance with which the philosopher is primarily concerned. That is to say, if a theory
satisfies an intellectual need, it is relevant for him. The number
of people who feel the intellectual needs which the philosopher
tries to satisfy is doubtless limited. But this has nothing to do
with the matter. The philosopher is not concerned with satisfying biological needs, nor even emotive needs. Still, it is undoubtedly true that a theory can hardly be intellectually satisfactory if it is indistinguishable from an alleged contrary theory.

One way of showing the intellectual relevance of theistic
philosophy would be to argue that it has a greater coordinating
and synthesising power than an atheistic world-view. If it can
be shown, that is to say, that a theistic world-view is more able
to coordinate the various forms of human experience or, if preferred, different language-games, in terms of an overall pattern
than is an atheist world-view, the relevance of theism would be
exhibited for those who feel the need for a coordinating overall
pattern. Again, a philosopher might take as his point of departure something which is widely recognised as relevant and
important, say the recognition of ideals, and then try to show
that in some real sense what is considered important and relevant demands or leads into what has at first been declared
unimportant and irrelevant.

To develop these ideas, however, would involve working out
a whole philosophy and considering possible objections. And I
cannot attempt this task here, even if I could fulfil it at all.
Instead I turn now to a necessarily very brief discussion of a
somewhat different question. If the theologian wishes to exhibit
the relevance of religious beliefs with the aid of ideas taken from
modern philosophy, where, if anywhere, will he find what he
needs?

VII

It is obvious that the theologian cannot get much help on
this matter from logical positivism. The logical positivist might
indeed say that talk about God is relevant for those who experience certain emotions and feel the need for this sort of
emotive language. But he would be likely to say this in a tone of
voice, so to speak, which would not be agreeable to the theologian. As for logical analysis, considered as an activity which

F

does not involve positivist presuppositions, the analyst can say that talk about God is relevant for anyone for whom it is a *living* language. But this is pretty well a tautology. To go much further than this the analyst would have to go outside the confines of logical analysis.

What then of existentialism?[19] Here we seem to have a more promising source of ideas which might be of help to the theologian. In fact, as we all know, some theologians, notably Professor Bultmann, have used ideas taken from this source.[20]

If we consider the atheist existentialism of Jean-Paul Sartre, we can see, I think, that, somewhat paradoxically, it underlines the importance and relevance of the problem of God. Sartre has indeed said that it makes no difference whether God exists or not, meaning apparently that, even if God does exist, man is still free, free even to defy God, as Orestes defies Zeus in *Les Mouches*. But Sartre has also said that his existentialism is nothing else but an attempt to draw all the logical conclusions from a consistently held atheist position.[21] And from atheism he concludes that things are 'gratuitous', that the world is without meaning or goal, that there are no absolute values and no universally obligatory moral law, that everything is permitted, and that man himself is *une passion inutile*, a useless striving.[22] Man is confronted with a meaningless world, and there is no one outside him on whom he can throw the responsibility for what happens in the world or for his own actions.

Now it is sometimes said that Christian writers who appeal to existentialist utterances about the meaningfulness of the world and use ideas such as that of 'dread' or 'anguish' are engaged in exploiting man's weakness, even in trying to reduce him to despair, with a view to persuading him to embrace religion. But Sartre is certainly not trying to reduce people to despair, to a perpetual feeling of *angoisse*. He is trying to get them to see what he believes to be the truth about the world in order that they may understand that it is man himself who gives meaning to the world and who creates values. It would be quite possible to state Sartre's philosophy without any of the emotive overtones which appear in his writings. Similarly, the theologian who uses ideas taken from atheist existentialism is not necessarily trying to make people thoroughly miserable, in order that he may more easily encourage wishful thinking. If he believes that the conclusions which Sartre derives from atheism do in fact follow from atheism, it is sufficient that he should emphasise their importance. For if the conclusions which follow from atheism are important for man, the concept of God too must possess importance. The theologian can perfectly well use atheist existentialism to illustrate the importance, and so the relevance, of the idea of God without trying to arouse and play upon the feeling of despair.

In any case the pertinent question is whether the conclusions which Sartre derives from atheism do in fact follow from it. To me it seems pretty obvious that if the world and human life and history can be said to have a goal or end or 'meaning' other than the meaning attributed by man himself, this goal or end or 'meaning' must be determined from outside, as it were. But the relation of ethics to religious belief is a more complicated matter, and I cannot discuss it here. I simply wish to point out that if the theologian believes that on atheist premises the world is as writers such as Sartre and Camus represent it as being, he has every right to use this idea of the world as a means of showing that the question of God is not a merely trivial question, devoid of any importance or consequences.

To illustrate the importance of the problem of God is not, however, quite the same thing as to show that there is a God. And Sartre, as we have noted, has maintained that there cannot be a God inasmuch as the concept of God is self-contradictory. But I do not myself think that this argument to show that the concept of God is self-contradictory is cogent.[23] It is true that we find Sartre writing in *Situations* in 1947 that 'God is dead, but man has not for all that become atheistic. Silence of the transcendent joined to the permanence of the need for religion in modern man—that is still the major thing, today as yesterday!'[24] But I should not wish to lay emphasis on this passage, as in later writings Sartre has stated that he is quite certain of the truth of atheism. Perhaps the most one can say is that atheist existentialism can serve to illustrate the importance of the idea of God. Whether it makes a man wish that there were a God, is another question. It would hardly have this effect with those who claim that God must die in order that man may come into his own.

By emphasising man's contingency Sartre draws attention to

one of the situations which Jaspers describes as limit-situations. And according to Jaspers it is in confrontation with these situations that man transcends towards and can become aware of the all-encompassing presence of the hidden ultimate reality. Jaspers himself finds a tension between 'philosophical faith', for which God is always a hidden mystery which can be conceived only in terms of symbols, none of which are final, and Christian faith in God as uniquely revealed in Christ. But the theologian can of course argue that the existentialist analysis or analyses of man leads to an opening up of the problem of God, while he goes on to argue that God issues out of the darkness which surrounds him only through self-disclosure or self-manifestation.

It must be admitted of course that when people suggest that talk about God is irrelevant, they are suggesting that Christianity is irrelevant for the life in the modern world of the business man, the workman, the policeman and so on. And remarks about limit-situations and a hidden Transcendent would seem to them to be beside the point. But to exhibit the relevance of Christianity in the way envisaged is not the philosopher's job. All that I have been suggesting is that if the theologian wishes to use ideas taken from modern philosophy as a help in showing the relevance of the concept of revelation, in the sense of divine self-disclosure, he can do worse than turn to existentialism, inasmuch as the existentialists who are open to the idea of God leave him hidden, so to speak, as far as philosophy is concerned, without attempting a dogmatic imposition of positive concepts of God to rival the Christian conception.

5
The philosophical relevance of mysticism

WHEN the philosopher turns to the study of religion, he is confronted by what William James called 'the varieties of religious experience', and by claims of having encountered or experienced God or the Absolute. These are of course empirical data. That is to say, it is an empirical fact that some people at any rate have had experiences which are customarily described as religious. And it is an empirical fact that some people have claimed to have enjoyed union with or experience of God. These phenomena are not of course coextensive with religion. But they are among the data which offer themselves to the philosopher of religion as material for attention and reflection.

Now there is more than one way in which the philosopher can interest himself in religious experience. For example, he might be primarily interested in it from a phenomenological point of view. He might attempt to disentangle different types of religious experience and to provide descriptive analyses of them, so far as this is possible. Or he might be primarily interested in the matter from the point of view of logical or conceptual analysis. He might try to discover, for instance, whether or not common use of the term 'religious experience' implies any necessary and sufficient conditions for describing an experience as 'religious'. But in whatever way he approaches the subject, the question is likely to occur to his mind whether the ascertainable empirical data provide a basis for inferring the existence of God. The philosopher obviously cannot be expected to accept without more ado claims of having encountered or experienced God, even when he has no reason for doubting the sincerity of the person who makes the claim. For the philosopher is well aware that people can sincerely believe that they have seen or felt something objectively existing 'out there' and yet be mistaken. I do not think that there is any need to labour this point. It is clear, however, that in the case of the man who claims to see pink snakes in the room or an oasis in the desert, there are ways of ascertaining whether he is or is not mistaken in his interpretation of his experience. Is there any analogous way of checking the claim of the man who says that he has encountered or experienced a divine reality? If there is a way of showing that the claim is valid, we have an empirically-based proof of the existence of God. If there is not, the claim may indeed be valid in point of fact, but there is not way of showing that it is valid.

II

At this point I wish to make some clarificatory remarks, in order to delimit the area of discussion.

i) In the first place nobody, so far as I know, has presented the argument from religious experience to the existence of God as a strict logical demonstration. It seems to me that the argument could be turned into a logical demonstration only by begging the whole question—by defining, that is to say, religious experience as experience of God. In this case to assert the occurrence of religious experience would be to assert the existence of God. The whole point at issue, however, is whether there *is* religious experience in this sense. So unless we propose to beg the question from the start, we have to take as our point of departure types of experience which are not defined from the outset as experience of God.

ii) It is thus a question of considering the relevant data and deciding on the most reasonable explanation. In this situation there is of course plenty of room for the influence of presuppositions and bias. But this state of affairs cannot be altered by decree. All that we can do is to consider the topic as dispassionately and objectively as possible. This may mean that the ensuing discussion is rather high-and-dry or academic. But it is not the job of the philosopher of religion to edify people, nor, for the matter of that, to disedify them.

iii) Now I have spoken of 'the argument from religious experience'. What is to count as religious experience? I do not think that any very clear limits can be set. For example, there are certain types of experience which some might call aesthetic and others religious, while others would say that there are experiences which are frequently described as aesthetic but which at the same time may exemplify the sense of the numinous which Rudolf Otto found at the basis of religion.[1] In the circumstances therefore I propose to make a terminological decision: I propose, for the purpose of this discussion, to mean by religious experience primarily mysticism. My reason is that it seems to me that the persuasiveness of the argument from religious experience grows in proportion to the strength of the *prima facie* case for saying that a person is acted upon or caught up into union with a reality immeasurably greater than himself. And it is mysticism especially which exemplifies this sort of case.

iv) It ought to be made clear, however, that in speaking of mysticism I am not referring to phenomena such as imaginative visions, voices, levitation or even to ecstasies and raptures considered under their physical or corporeal aspects. We all know that some people 'see things' and hear voices without any even *prima facie* connection with intimate union with God. And there can certainly be pathological states resembling ecstasy which are susceptible of a purely naturalistic explanation. In referring to mysticism I am speaking primarily of states in which the subject is aware (at least in the subjective sense of awareness) of being acted upon, of an intimate uniting and one-ing with a Being immeasurably greater than himself and which is felt to be in some sense the 'really real', the ultimate reality.

v) Finally, how do I understand the word 'God', in the first instance at least? I understand the term 'God', in the first instance, in a minimal sense. By it I mean a reality which is transcendent, in the sense that it is identifiable neither with the empirical world as it appears to us in everyday experience and in natural science nor with the finite self considered as such; and I mean a reality which is thought to be the ultimate reality and the ground, in some sense, of the existence of the plurality of finite things.

As this minimal concept of God would more or less cover one of the main Hindu conceptions of the Absolute, I wish to add the following two points.

(*a*) I am quite well aware of the view (indeed I agree with it) that there are different types of what is commonly called 'mysticism', and that one type may consist in an experience of the naked self, so to speak, which, deprived of all characteristics, is indistinguishable from any other self. If there is such a type of experience, it would help to explain the idea of the one *atman*. And it would not necessarily have anything to do with what is ordinarily meant by God.

(*b*) At the same time I am certainly not prepared to restrict mystical experience of God to Christians. I do not see why a Hindu should not enjoy mystical experience. But if he does, he will interpret it of course in terms of Hindu metaphysics.

III

This last remark brings me to a point which is perhaps a commonplace, but which is too important to be passed over. The point is this. What a mystic says about his experience is always an interpretation subsequent to the experience itself. And it is clear that any mystic tends to interpret his experience in terms of his pre-existing beliefs. Obviously, this holds good for the Christian as well as for the Hindu or the Moslem.

The point can indeed be exaggerated. That is to say, we cannot exclude the possibility of a man being led by mystical experience to change, modify or deepen his previous beliefs. Thus it seems true to say that Sufi mysticism, where influential, reacted in a fairly marked manner on the Moslem concept of God and of man's relation to him. Generally speaking, however, we expect a mystic to interpret his experience in terms of an already existing framework of interpretation. What else indeed can he do?

Needless to say, the testimony of those who lay claim to mystical experience is not all on the same level. Even those who are convinced that there can be, and has been, mystical knowledge of an objectively existing divine reality, allow for a distinction between genuine mystics, deluded persons and bogus mystics or frauds. There are some cases of course where we have sufficient knowledge of the lives and characters of mystics to be able to use quite ordinary criteria to decide whether they were simply mad or whether they were likely to be saying what they themselves knew to be false. But though there are doubtless some mystical writers whose sincerity cannot reasonably be called in question, it still remains true that the interpretation which they give of their experience is in terms of pre-existing beliefs. Hence we cannot demand that the mystic's account of his experience should be accepted simply on his own authority.

IV

Now if what I have been saying is true, it follows that we cannot, simply by reading the writings of mystics, arrive at 'pure experience', at uninterpreted experience that is to say. Hence any argument from mysticism to the existence of God must proceed, I think, on the following lines.

If in the case of mystics belonging to different historical periods and cultures we can find some basic agreement, in spite of all differences between their accounts of their experience, it is more reasonable and more in accordance with an open-minded 'empiricism' to take seriously their claims to have experienced a divine reality than not to do so. Further, if the mystic's recorded experience tends to follow the path which one would expect it to follow if there were a transcendent divine reality and if man could have knowledge by acquaintance of this reality, this fact tends to confirm the validity of the mystic's claim.

In regard to inquiry into the measure of agreement which can be found among the mystics, there are indeed a number of points to bear in mind, The wider we extend the application of the term 'mystic', the greater become the differences between their utterances. Hence there is the danger of narrowing down or restricting application of the term in such a way as to diminish these differences in advance, thus enabling us to find the sort of agreement which we are seeking. Indeed, some might question whether any real measure of agreement among mystical writers can be found, except through the policy of selective attention or of being very choosy in our admission of people to the class of mystics.

Though, however, this is a real danger, and though there are, in my view, different types of mysticism, most people, I suppose, would be prepared to grant that in different periods of history and in different cultures we can find some mystics who have claimed to have experienced a union of the most intimate kind with what is taken spontaneously to be the ultimate reality, regarded as transcendent in at any rate a minimal sense of the term. Even the Hindu mystic does not identify the Absolute simply with the world of multiplicity as given in ordinary experience, nor with the finite human self considered simply as such. It is arguable at least that we can in fact find a quite impressive measure of agreement, without having to deny the existence of different types or kinds of mysticism.

Now it is true that the comparative rarity of mystical experience produces an understandable bias against accepting the testimony of mystical writers as evidence for the existence of God as a transcendent reality. After all, most of us derive our knowledge of mysticism from descriptive accounts. And even if confirming statistics are not available, we can safely assume, I think, that in comparison with the number of those who have enjoyed mystical experience the number of those who have written accounts which have come down to us is small. Hence the field of investigation is admittedly pretty limited. And anyone who holds that we can know of the existence of things only through sense-experience and through empirical veri-fication of hypotheses which can be construed as predictions of possible sensory experience, is unlikely to give serious attention to the idea of mystical knowledge.

The retort can always be made, however, that if the theory of knowledge just alluded to is proposed as the provisional result of an examination of the ways in which we actually acquire knowledge of reality, the proponent of the theory should be prepared to give serious consideration to phenomena which, at first sight at least, show that the theory is too narrow. If he is not prepared to do this, he manifests a narrow-minded dog-matism. Not all people see or hear equally well. Why should there not be people who enjoy knowledge by acquaintance of a transcendent reality? If mystics are few in number, this is not surprising. We are embodied spirits. Our attention is naturally directed to the visible and tangible world about us. We are naturally inclined to think that, as the saying goes, seeing is believing. But to insist that no other path to knowledge is possible is unwarranted dogmatism.

It may be said of course that neither mystical experience nor anything else can contribute in the slightest degree to proving the existence of a transcendent reality which it would be appropriate to call God. For 'to exist' means to be in principle a possible object of sense-experience. It is therefore nonsense to talk about the existence of a reality which cannot in principle be the object of sense-experience. This is why the mystic's claims cannot be entertained, and why a naturalistic explanation of his psychological experiences must be sought.

This contention seems to me to be a sophisticated and misleading way of giving expression to an assumed theory of being or metaphysics. It is misleading to the extent that it endeavours to draw a veil over its ontological or metaphysical character by an appeal to ordinary language. And the point to notice is that it is precisely the validity of this theory of being or metaphysics which is called in question by the mystic's claim. Hence to refute the claim by reiterating the theory challenged by the claim is a clear example of unwarranted dogmatism.

Now if we assume the existence of a transcendent God, it seems that any direct approach to him would involve a passing beyond or transcending of all that is not God. But it is precisely the things which are not God which are seen, heard and felt and which normally constitute the objects of attention, desire and so on. To pass beyond them in the direction of the Transcendent therefore would involve entry into a darkness or night. And if the mystic came out the other side, so to speak, and enjoyed a realised state of union with God, this state would hardly be describable in terms of a language tailored to quite other uses.

Of course, when I suggest that this is the sort of thing which we might expect, if there were a transcendent God, I may be indulging in hindsight, as a result of some acquaintance with a number of mystical writings. However this may be, the kind of itinerary which I have outlined is certainly to be found in the works of, say, St John of the Cross, who dwells at length on the 'dark night' in its various phases and who openly acknowledges the difficulty encountered in trying to give any idea at all of the higher mystical states to those who have not experienced them.

v

Now this sort of argument can doubtless be presented in a persuasive way. But serious objections can be raised. And I wish to develop one of them briefly.

Let us assume, as I think that we must assume, that the occurrence of mystical experiences, considered as psychological events, does not entail the existence of God in such a way that we would be involved in self-contradiction if we admitted the occurrence of the events and yet denied the existence of God. In this case more than one explanation of the experiences is logically possible. And if this is granted, it is open to anyone to argue that we ought always to prefer a naturalistic explanation to one which involves postulating a supernatural reality. For if a naturalistic explanation is forthcoming, a supernatural explanation becomes superfluous.

In addition it can be urged that even if a satisfactory naturalistic explanation of mystical experience is not available here and now, we cannot exclude in advance the possibility of one being found in the future. Hence even if we did accept a supernatural explanation, it should be on a purely provisional basis, which is not a very promising foundation for belief in God.

In point of fact some writers (J. H. Leuba was one of them) have maintained that there is no factor discoverable in mystical experience which cannot be explained naturalistically in terms of the operation of physiological and psychological causes. It may well be the case that it is the feeling of being acted upon, of being taken up into a unity or of being filled with light and love which makes the mystic see in such phenomena effects of the divine action. But the feeling of 'givenness', of being acted upon, accompanies the emergence of psychical processes from the infraconscious into consciousness. So it has been maintained. To take a simple example, a pious person may be troubled by conflicts, ideas and temptations which seem to come from outside, to thrust themselves upon him without his choice and against his will; and he attributes them to diabolical agency or suggestion. But the psycholanalyst may be able to reveal the origins of these phenomena in the infraconscious. Hence the feeling of 'givenness' provides no proof that mystical experience is what the mystic believes it to be.

To this line of argument the reply has sometimes been made that even if a purely psychological account of mystical experience can or could be given, it by no means necessarily follows that the mystic's account of the matter is false. Naturalistic explanations can obviously be given of, for example, the movements of the planets. But the Christian at any rate does not suppose that this fact excludes the divine activity in Nature. Similarly, it might be true both that a naturalistic account of mystical experience can be given and that the experience is in fact what the mystic believes it to be.[2] The languages, psychological and religious, may be complementary rather than mutually exclusive, though one should not use both at the same time.

This reply may be true as far as it goes. But it is not, I think, of much help in the immediate context. If a Christian attributes the movements of the planets to God, he does not do so as a result of inspecting the planets' movements but because he believes, on other grounds, that everything at every moment depends existentially on God. For the moment, however, I am concerned with the idea of arguing to the existence of God on the sole basis of mystical experience. And if an adequate explanation of mystical experience were forthcoming, the argument to the existence of God, in this narrowly conceived form of the argument that is to say, would be ruled out.

VI

Here perhaps some reference should be made to the claim that mystical experiences can be produced artificially by the use of certain drugs. In this matter I must confess to being in the perhaps disadvantageous position of having no first-hand knowledge of the effects of mescalin, LSD and so on, but only of tobacco. However, as I am not a St John of the Cross or a St Teresa, I am in much the same case in regard to their sublime experiences. In both cases I can go only by what I have read. But read I can. And it seems pretty clear to me that descriptions of the states attained through the use of drugs do not tally with what a writer such as St John of the Cross has to say about what be considers his most significant and important experiences. It seems undeniable that certain drugs can produce a peculiar vision of the familiar world, corresponding to part at least of what Professor W. T. Stace called 'extrovert' mysticism.[3] It also seems clear that certain drugs can produce a feeling or conviction—call it what you will—that all selves are one self. But I doubt, very much whether it can be successfully maintained that there is any real evidence for the production by the use of drugs of what St John of the Cross describes as the transforming union with God, which is not a passing occurrence such as ecstasy but has a profound effect on a man's whole life. However, I admit that if it could be shown that the use of drugs was capable of producing fit candidates for canonisation, one would have to reconsider the matter.

VII

In any case it is arguable that even if a naturalistic explanation of the highest mystical states was possible, we could never *know* that it was adequate. For the highest mystical states are admitted by the mystics themselves to be inexpressible. And if we accept this account of the matter, it seems to me that we could never know that a valid and adequate purely naturalistic explanation had been given, for the simple reason that we would not really know what we were talking about. For the same reason we could not know that states produced by drugs were comparable to the supreme experiences of the mystics.

Some writers, such as Professor J. N. Findlay,[4] have maintained that we cannot take seriously what the mysics say about ineffability. For even if mystical states are difficult to describe and to understand, the mystics have in fact succeeded in writing a good deal about them.

There can, however, be some misunderstanding here. If, for example, St John of the Cross refers to an incommunicable mystical knowledge of God, he is obviously not referring to a knowledge *that*, a knowledge expressed in propositions about God. He does not mean that the mystic has new information about God, secrets which would be in principle communicable to others. He is referring to a knowing-God, a knowledge by acquaintance. And his point is that this knowledge is so different from our knowledge of perceptible things that it cannot really be understood except by the few people who have personal experience of it. If it is asked why, in this case, St John of the Cross writes about the matter at all, the answer is fairly simple. He writes for those who are already devoted to the inner spiritual life, and he puts before them a kind of map, not with the idea that they can then understand everything in advance but so that, if they make progress, they may recognise stages as they come to them and not think that they have strayed into forbidden territory or are suffering from self-deception. For those accustomed only to ordinary discursive meditation on religious truths, the mystical life, including the dark night, will seem strange and perplexing. The saint wishes to reassure them, even though he knows that they cannot understand in advance what they have never experienced. He is also writing for those spiritual directors who are inclined to think that anything outside the range of ordinary piety is dangerous illusion and who try to clip the wings of potential mystics. Let these directors learn at any rate that there are ranges of spiritual experience beyond their ken.

Perhaps therefore we can take what mystical writers have said about ineffability rather more seriously than some people do. It must be added, however, that if ignorance of the nature of the higher mystical states disqualifies a man from claiming that he has given an adequate explanation of them in naturalistic terms, the same ignorance disqualifies anyone from using such states as a premise for proving the existence of God. What is sauce for the goose is sauce for the gander.

VIII

At the same time we cannot simply dismiss what Professor Findlay says. We can get a pretty good idea, I think, of the initial stages of the mystical life; and even if the highest stages cannot really be understood from outside, it is not unreasonable to claim that by the use of images, analogies and paradoxial utterances mystical writers succeed in conveying some sort of notion of what they are talking about. In this case the possibility of argument returns.

What kind of an argument, however, can it be? One might perhaps feel inclined to offer the existence of God as an explanatory hypothesis. But what would count as verification? The point of issue, it must be remembered, is whether certain mystical experiences are and can be shown to be experiences of God. Or, if we accept the statement of some mystics that they are aware of God in his action within the soul rather than directly of God himself, the point at issue is whether it can be shown that the experiences in question are caused by God. We cannot therefore propose the existence of God as a hypothesis and then, without more ado, offer future mystical experience as verification of the hypothesis. For the question is precisely whether such experiences do in fact constitute verification of the existence of God. Suppose that I were to propose the hypothesis that sudden deaths are due to the intervention of an evil genius. If someone then asked me for verifying or confirming evidence and I offered future sudden deaths as constituting the required verification, he might wonder whether I was joking or whether I was simply lacking in mental acumen.

We might of course introduce the idea of eschatological verification, by referring to what Christian theologians have called the beatific vision of God. As by definition the beatific vision is the immediate vision of God himself, anyone who embraced the hypothesis of God's existence and then, after death, came to enjoy the beatific vision, would find his hypothesis verified. This seems to me to be true. At the same time we could hardly expect an atheist to adopt the hypothesis of God's existence as a result of being offered as verification a Christian belief which he does not accept and which he perhaps regards as a piece of fantasy.

If therefore we are looking for a proof of the existence of God which is based simply on records of mystical experience, I doubt very much whether such a proof can be found. As I have already indicated, it is only by begging the whole question (by *defining* mystical experience as experience of God) that we can construct a logical demonstration. And if we do not beg the question in advance, and proceed by way of excluding alternative explanations of mystical experience, it is difficult to see how we can exclude the possibility of a naturalistic explanation in a sufficiently conclusive manner to warrant our bringing an accusation of irrationality or sheer prejudice against the man who says that psychology, as it develops, may very well succeed in providing an adequate explanation of mysticism and that he prefers to await such a development rather than, to accept a supernaturalistic explanation.

IX

At the same time it seems to me clear that a good many people do in fact feel that religious experience offers impres-

sive evidence of God's existence. Indeed, it is possible to recognise the weakness of the argument as I have proposed it and
yet to feel that mysticism offers impressive testimony to the
existence of God. Why do people feel in this way? One obvious
reason might be that a man can be predisposed by his pre-
existing beliefs to see in religious experience, especially in
mystical experience, confirmation of these beliefs. If, for
example, a man already believes in a personal God, he is likely
to envisage the possibility of man's entering into a personal
relationship with God and of his encountering God in some
sense of the term 'encounter'. For we can hardly conceive God
in terms of the analogy of personality without also envisaging
the possibility of an encounter with God analogous to encounter between human persons. Hence the believer in a
personal God is predisposed to see in religious experience in
general some degree of meeting with God and in mystical
experience in particular something analogous to intimate
personal relationships between human beings.

Similarly, the Hindu who is already convinced that there is
ultimately only one reality, the Absolute or Brahman, is predisposed to see in mysticism the realisation by the finite self of
its basic unity with the One.

At this point it may be as well for me to explain that I have
purposely chosen a rather weak word, 'predisposed', avoiding
the word 'predetermined'. For I have no intention of suggesting
that a man who already believes in God is *predetermined* to
interpret mystical experiences as confirmation of his belief.
It is quite possible, for example, for a man to believe in God
and at the same time to emphasise the divine transcendence in
such a way that he is not only suspicious of but also definitely
hostile to the claims made by mystics, and consequently welcomes attempts to explain mysticism naturalistically. This is
not a possibility thought up by myself. I have met one or two
convinced Moslems, for instance, who looked on mysticism with
definite hostility and apparently thought the Sufis unorthodox.
This view is not shared by all Moslems of course. But the
attitude is a real possibility. Indeed, it is by no means all
Christians who are favourable disposed towards mysticism.
Some Christians certainly think that mysticism expresses a self-
centred turning-away from this world and man's obligations to

G

it. They feel that what Plotinus described as 'the flight of the alone to the Alone'⁵ is not at all what is wanted of the Christian living in the modern world. I do not mention this view of the matter to endorse it, but rather to explain why I have carefully avoided words such as 'determined' or 'predetermined'.

Having made this point, I can now proceed to recall the view which I put forward earlier, that real belief in God rests on and is sustained by religious experience. I think that it is true to say that if a man already believes in a personal God, he is predisposed, other things being equal, to believe in the possibility of encounter with God, and is therefore predisposed to see in religious experience confirmation of his belief. But it is not sufficient to say this, even if it is true. For if real belief in God rests on what can fairly be described as religious experience, it is much easier to understand why a man should see in records of mystical experience confirmation of his belief. For he can see in such records accounts of experiences which go beyond anything which he has himself experienced but which none the less bear sufficient similarity to his own for him to be able to see these accounts as strengthening his belief in the possibility of encounter with God.

This might very well apply to the man who has the sort of experience, in confrontation with the limit-situations, of which Karl Jaspers speaks. That is to say, we can envisage a man who feels sure that there is some all-encompassing ultimate reality, some ultimate ground of finite existence, but who is not prepared to state definitely that he believes in God. In mystical experience such a man might see a testimony which strengthens his own belief. Further, he might see in records of mystical experience a key to the nature of the ultimate reality. A lot depends of course on what kind of mystical writings he reads. But it is possible, for example, for a man to see in mysticism a warrant for conceiving the ultimate reality as creative love.

When therefore I speak of a man being predisposed by his pre-existing belief to see in mysticism confirmation of his belief, I am not thinking simply of belief, apart, that is to say, from the personal experience which sustains it. Nor am I thinking simply of the man who would classify himself as an adherent of a definite religion, such as Christianity, Judaism or Islam.

X

Now I shall be told of course that what I have done is to offer a possible psychological explanation why some people find the argument from religious experience impressive, even perhaps when they are aware of the logical difficulties. But this psychological explanation, it will be said, does nothing to support the argument. It is a psychological explanation of a psychological state of mind and not a logical justification of an argument. To say, for instance, that real belief in God is itself sustained by religious experience may be to say what is true. But it does not show that the experience warrants the belief, from a logical point of view.

It is doubtless true that I have been offering a primarily psychological explanation of what seems to me to be a fact, namely that it is possible to recognise the weakness of the argument from religious experience, as I outlined it, and yet to remain profoundly dissatisfied and to feel that there is something more in the argument than I have allowed for. But there might very well be another reason too, namely that the argument as hitherto discussed appears too narrow and circumscribed. Surely, it may be said, the argument from religious experience gains in strength when it constitutes simply one strand in a much wider line of thought, when it forms part of a series of lines of thought converging towards a comprehensive world-view.

The philosophy of Henri Bergson provides an example of the sort of thing I have in mind. In *Creative Evolution* Bergson interpreted evolution as a creative process manifesting the immanent activity of a dynamic principle or energy or life-force which he called God. Later, in *The Two Sources of Morality and Religion*, he published the results of his reflections on the history of religion and religious experience. One can say, I think, that he saw the history of religion as a kind of stream, often shallow, often muddy, in which mysticism represents the deep pools. In Christian mysticism in particular, and in the mystical experience of those who had been influenced to some degree by Christianity, he saw the irruption of a divine love, overflowing the confines of what he called 'static religion'. This idea of mysticism then reacts on the earlier concept of creative life. 'God is love, and the object of love: herein lies the whole con-

tribution of mysticism.'⁶ Bergson thus uses mysticism not to
prove the existence of God in the first instance but to throw
light on the divine nature.

It has been said of Bergson that he was not addicted to providing reasons, either good or bad, for the views which he
invited his readers to accept, but that he relied 'on a certain
poetic quality in his illustrations'.⁷ It can also be objected
that his account of religion in general and of mysticism in
particular lies open to serious criticism. However, though I do
not think that even Bergson's warmest admirers could successfully claim that precise analytic thinking was his strong point,⁸
it seems to me an exaggeration to suggest that he offered no
reasons, whether good or bad, for his philosophical theories. In
any case I mention his thought simply as an example of a philosophy which grew up, so to speak, or developed through he
convergence of a variety of lines of reflection, among which
reflection on mysticism had a place. The philosophy of Bergson
is not a closely-knit system of a take-it-or-leave-it kind. It
presents, through the convergence of several lines of thought,
a general vision of the world.

A philosopher might of course start at the other end. That
is to say, he might presuppose the existence of God and try to
show how a theistic world-vision is capable of accommodating
within itself the forms of human experience and the aspects of
reality which other world-visions take account of, and that, in
addition, it makes better sense of certain forms of experience,
such as religious experience, than can be made by a non-
theistic world-vision.⁹

One may perhaps be inclined to speak of exhibiting a
pattern. I have done so on occasion. But there is need for some
care here. It is obviously sometimes possible to get a man who
sees one pattern to see another. If a man sees the duck-rabbit as
a duck, we may succeed in getting him to see it as a rabbit. But
God is not simply phenomena as perceived in a certain way.
Hence it is not simply a matter of exhibiting a pattern, as one
might try to exhibit a pattern in what at first sight seems to be a
chaotic mass of dots on a piece of paper. Exhibition of a pattern
is one element. But it is not the only element. For the philosopher is presumably concerned with exhibiting a pattern as
warranting an inference. We might perhaps wish to say that

this is not necessarily the case. For may not the philosopher be concerned with exhibiting a pattern in the hope that it will provide the occasion for what Dr I. T. Ramsey, Bishop of Durham, calls a 'disclosure'? The question arises, however, whether the experience of something beng 'disclosed' does not express an implicit inference.[10]

However this may be, a philosopher can employ reflection on mysticism, as well as on other factors, in an attempt to commend a certain world-vision. And we can endeavour to find criteria for judging between rival world-visions. Some writers have suggested, for example, internal coherence and comprehensiveness as criteria. As for internal coherence, even those philosophers who speak of the world as meaningless presumably try to achieve internal consistency in their account of the meaningless world. They try, for instance, to avoid making statements which imply that the world has a meaning in a sense in which, as they maintain, it has no meaning. As for comprehensiveness, we might take it that, other things being equal, a general conceptual scheme or world-vision[11] which is capable of accommodating within itself without distortion a greater range of types of human experience or of recognised aspects of the world is to be preferred to one which is more restricted in its scope or which is not able to accommodate certain sets of data without distortion or an unjustified reductionism.[12]

Obviously, the application of such criteria is by no means plain sailing. If, for example, we talk about a given world-vision as making 'better sense' of religious experience than another world-vision, what precisely do we understand by 'making sense'? Do we understand the phrase in a question-begging manner? Again, some criteria demand other criteria. For instance, though an 'unjustified reductionism' is clearly something to avoid, what is the criterion for use of the word 'unjustified'? None the less, it seems possible to argue about the persuasiveness of different world-visions.[13] And reference to and reflection on mysticism may form an element in the argument.

XI

If this discussion appears somewhat arid, there is a possible reason to be borne in mind. When a man is profoundly impressed by accounts of religious experience, seen in the context of lives of outstanding quality, it may very well be the case that his reading is for him a means whereby a personal awareness of the reality and presence of God is mediated. The awareness of God can be mediated in many ways, for some by what we call the voice of conscience, for others by beauty, for others by the lives and experience of outstanding religious figures. It is natural that the philosopher should interpret these people's mental processes in terms of inferences, and that he should then question the validity of these inferences. But discussion of the validity or invalidity of the inferences is likely to seem arid and artificial to the man who feels that he has in some sense (a sense which he may be quite unable to define) become aware of the presence or the reality of God. In the case of mysticism a man may be conscious of the fact that the experience described transcends the range of his own experience; and yet at the same time his reading and effort of understanding may be for him the occasion of a personal awareness of God. Whether there can be an awareness of what Kant called the 'supersensible' probably cannot be *proved*. But neither can it be *disproved*, except in terms of question-begging presuppositions.

A final remark. Nothing of course that I have said here is intended to belittle religious experience in general or mysticism in particular. I have been discussing *arguments* from religious experience to the existence of God, not the value of mysticism. And I wish to emphasise the fact that even if, in my opinion, the usefulness of mysticism for the apologetic purpose of proving God's existence to atheists is pretty limited, I consider that reflection on mysticism can be of great value for religion. A recent writer has said that 'squeamishness about anthropomorphism, at root, is embarrassment about what makes real religion possible'.[14] One sees what he means of course, namely that if we try to purify our concept of God of all that cannot be literally predicated of him, the concept tends to become deprived of all content 'for finite human thinkers',[15] and that then, for many people and possibly for everybody most of the time, it cannot fulfil the functions in religious life which are fulfilled by analogies and images. At the same time it seems to be important for religion that we should not forget that what such analogies refer to in God himself transcends our grasp. Reflection on mysticism can remind us of this. It can serve as a valuable correctve to any tendency to think of God as a large-scale human being. At the same time mysticism also reminds us that the divine transcendence does not entail a spatial gap between God and us, nor a yawning chasm that is unbridgeable by love.

Part II

6
Metaphysics today

THE accusation has sometimes been brought against the philosophers who represent the prevailing style of philosophising in this country that they occupy themselves with trivial inquiries and leave aside broad problems about reality as a whole and about the ultimate significance of human life and history. I do not think that it is true to say that the linguistic or logical analysts[1] have abandoned any attempt to understand better the world or human experience. A preoccupation with the minute and detailed mapping-out of different forms of locution may indeed give the impression of being a species of philosophical grammar which has no particular interest for the majority of people. But it seems to me quite clear that a study of so-called ordinary language can help us to see the view of things, the implicit philosophy, which is embodied in the concrete utterances of ordinary speech. It is as though the analyst said, for example: 'Let us get away from what the philosophers have said about man. Let us look at what man says about himself indirectly. That is, let us look at the view of man which is indirectly revealed in his ordinary speech.' This line of inquiry cannot properly be called trivial. Man's experience or consciousness of himself, as indirectly expressed in his language, is certainly philosophically relevant. At the very least it gives us some sort of a touchstone. For there is likely to be something wrong with any philosophical theory of man which is flatly incompatible with what we might call man's spontaneous awareness of himself. But though it seems to me absurd to write off all the work of the analysts as trivial, it remains true that the representative philosophers of the

95

movement are not notably troubled by what Mr G. J. Warnock calls 'cosmic anxieties'.[2] Their writings are not very evidently permeated by any spirit of dread or *Angst*.

The reply has been made to this objection that modern philosophers[3] are not particularly interested in problems of speculative metaphysics. Metaphysical speculation, it has been said, has often arisen from or been a substitute for religious or theological doctrine. But, as Professor Ryle has put it,[4] the theological fire has died down, and the kettle of theological philosophy cannot keep itself on the boil. We cannot force an interest in what does not interest us. And it is not desirable that we should feign an interest which we do not feel.

This line of reply is reasonable enough as far as it goes. We can no more demand of every philosopher that he should interest himself in metaphysics than that he should interest himself in moral philosophy or in the philosophy of aesthetics. But the statement that a given philosopher is not interested in metaphysics tells us something about the philosopher rather than about metaphysics. If I say that I am not interested in football and that I find the idea of prize-fighting repellent I am making an autobiographical statement. Of course, if we assume that I have any real knowledge of football and prize fighting, then anybody who had an intimate acquaintance with my psychological make-up could deduce that football and prize-fighting must possess certain characteristics if the one does not interest me and the other repels me. Similarly, if we assume that Mr X really understands what metaphysics is, then from his statement that he is not interested in metaphysics we could deduce something about it, provided that we possessed a sufficient psychological knowledge of Mr X for this purpose. But this would be an extremely roundabout way of approaching the subject of metaphysics, quite apart from any considerations of propriety and good manners. We have to focus our attention on what is said about metaphysics rather than on the individual who says it.

It has been held in some quarters that metaphysical questions cannot be answered, even in principle, because they are not genuine questions. The are the fruit of linguistic or logical confusion. Because I can quite properly ask for the explanation of a given event of phenomenon, I am inclined to suppose that

I can properly ask for the explanation of all events or phenomena. Because I can quite properly ask for the cause of a given occurrence, I am inclined to take it for granted that I can properly ask for the cause of all occurrences. Because I can quite properly inquire into the significance of this or that set of historical events, I may be prompted to ask for the significance of human history as a whole. Because I can ask why a person did this or that or why this or that happened,[5] I may feel inclined to ask why there is something rather than nothing. But in all such cases the meaning of certain terms is stretched to breaking-point. If I ask for the explanation of the failure of the electric light, the term 'explanation' has a definite meaning. I am asking for the empirical cause or causes of the event. But if I ask for the explanation of all events, the term loses this definite meaning, though the associations of the ordinary use of the term may obscure this nebulosity from view. Further, if I ask for the explanation of all events or for the cause of all phenomena, I tacitly complete the series and treat the world as a limited totality of which such a question can reasonably be asked. In Kantian language I have turned a heuristic idea of wholeness or totality into a constitutive idea.

In other words, metaphysical inquiries show that the inquirer does not understand the logic of our language.[6] They manifest a sort of mental malady or disease, and what is called for is not an attempt to answer the questions raised but a therapeutic treatment. The logical misunderstanding which gives rise to the questions or problems needs to be cleared up. The patient will then be cured of the tendency to raise metaphysical questions.

But will he? Not in all cases, it appears. It is an odd state of affairs when we find a philosopher admitting that though logic shows him that the question 'Why is there something rather than nothing?' is absurd he still wishes to ask the question and furthermore, feels that it is a question of tremendous importance and significance.[7] The treatment does not seem to have effected a cure, and one begins to wonder whether the diagnosis was correct. At any rate the malady appears to be deep-seated; linguistic bewitchment seems to exercise a powerful influence. And this is indeed what Wittgenstein says.

This theory of linguistic bewitchment can, however, be

developed in a way which involves a rather less negative attitude towards metaphysics. Thus according to Professor Wisdom the metaphysicians are accustomed to uttering paradoxes. And though these paradoxes are from one point of view absurd, they can serve a useful purpose. Let us suppose that I have been misled by the grammatical similarity between, say, 'lying is wrong' and 'daffodils are yellow' into thinking that normative ethical statements are of the same 'logical' type as empirical descriptive statements. Along comes the logical positivist of the old dogmatic variety (who, for Wisdom, is an unwitting metaphysician) and says: 'Normative ethical statements are meaningless; they are pseudo-propositions.' From one point of view his assertion is preposterous and absurd For there is an obvious sense in which we all know what normative ethical statements mean. At the same time the positivist's preposterous assertion can shock me into seeing what I had not noticed before, namely the difference between normative ethical statements and, say, the descriptive statements of empirical science. As Wittgenstein would say, 'A picture held us captive. And we could not get outside it, for it lay in our language and language seemed to repeat it to us inexorably.'[8] Well, a preposterous statement has shaken us up, and we have liberated ourselves. But then, of course, we can turn on the positivist and try to release him from his narrow and cramping 'picture'.

In other words, the utterances of metaphysicians, strange though they may be, can embody insights. Insights into what? Into what is in a sense already plain. 'The aspects of things that are most important for us are hidden because of their simplicity and familiarity.'[9] Examination of metaphysical paradoxes can help us to obtain '*a clear view* of the use of our words'.[10]

But metaphysical systems, it is now not uncommonly said, can do more than this. For they can enable us to see the world in different lights. Thus according to Dr F. Waismann 'at the living centre of every philosophy is a vision. . . . There is something visionary about great metaphysicians as if they had the power to see beyond the horizons of their time'.[11] This is a remarkable statement when one remembers that Dr Waismann was once Assistant to Moritz Schlick of the Vienna Circle. To be sure, Dr Waismann argues that the greatness of

Descartes consists in his vision of the comprehensibility of Nature and that his true successors are Newton and other natural scientists rather than Spinoza and Malebranche. But the point is that the old positivist notion of the meaninglessness of metaphysics is excluded. To say that metaphysics is nonsense is nonsense.[12]

On this view of metaphysics the value of a system seems to be estimated according to its effects—that is, according to the desirability or undesirability of the stimulus provided in a non-metaphysical field. This need not be natural science, of course. It might be the field of morals. Some pictures of the world may favour desirable conduct, others undesirable. True enough; but unless some cognitive value is attributed to metaphysics in itself, it is unlikely that anyone will put himself to the trouble of working out a metaphysical system. The metaphysicians did not elaborate their systems simply as intellectual games or as pleasing aesthetic wholes or even merely with a view to the effects which they might produce; they developed their systems because they considered them as certainly or at least as probably true. And while the present tolerant and respectful attitude towards original metaphysicians is all to the good, it is not by itself likely to produce a resurgence of metaphysics.

Metaphysics is not, of course, all of a piece. In a recent book Mr P. F. Strawson makes a distinction between 'revisionary' and 'descriptive' metaphysics, without, however, wishing to say that any metaphysical philosophy must belong exclusively to one of these categories.[13] Descriptive metaphysics explores and describes the latent actual structure of our thought about the world. That is to say, it describes the most general features of our conceptual structure. Kant's philosophy would be an example of his type of metaphysics. So would a great deal of the thought of Aristotle. Revisionary metaphysics, however, is concerned with changing our conceptual structure by producing a better one. Berkeley, for instance, tried to get us to see the world in a new light. Mr Strawson does not reject revisionary metaphysics as useless.[14] On the contrary, he speaks of the 'enduring philosophical utility' of its productions.[15] But he evidently thinks that it stands in greater need of justification than does descriptive metaphysics, which is concerned with the fundamentally unchanging conceptual structure of human thought and needs no justification 'beyond that of inquiry in general'.[16]

I have mentioned Mr Strawson because he is a prominent member of the younger generation of contemporary British philosophers. And his willingness to speak of his own line of inquiry as 'metaphysics' is symptomatic of the tolerant attitude towards metaphysics which is now fairly common. But I do not think that this attitude should be depicted as expressing a complete change of front on the part of the so-called analysts. It involves, of course, a rejection of the positivist attitude towards metaphysics. But the linguistic approach to philosophy is not at all the same thing as logical positivism, though it can, of course, be associated with it. Apart from the fact that thinkers such as G. E. Moore and Lord Russell were never logical positivists, logical or linguistic analysis, as I have already observed, need not take the form of a species of philosophical grammar. It can be used, and has been used, as an instrument for elucidating the concepts and views of reality implicitly expressed in ordinary language.[17] And it is no great step from the practice of this procedure in limited fields to the line of inquiry which Mr Strawson calls 'descriptive metaphysics'. Further, the concept of revisionary metaphysics is a natural complement to that of descriptive metaphysics.[18] Hence the attitude represented by Mr Strawson seems to me to constitute a development of an existing line of thought rather than any radical change of front.

What I have been saying in this section is familiar enough to those who keep abreast of the philosophical writing of this country, though I have no doubt that what I have said could have been much better expressed. But there are doubtless many people who assume that British philosophy as a whole is not only unmetaphysical (which is, I think a fair description) but also positively anti-metaphysical, in the sense that most representative British philosophers are persuaded that metaphysics is necessarily sheer nonsense or meaningless balderdash. And anyone who has this conception of British philosophy might expect that an English philosopher who proposes as I do to develop some lines of metaphysical reflection would begin by attacking logical positivism and arguing that metaphysics can be meaningful. But there is no need to attack logical positivism in its virulently anti-metaphysical form. For in this form it is a past episode. In the present climate of thought a philosopher can quite well develop some metaphysical reflections without the uneasy feeling that a logical positivist is looking over his shoulder the whole time, exclaiming 'Nonsense!' One's views may indeed be judged to be nonsense, but, if so, it will not be, generally speaking, simply because they are metaphysical. What is required of the would-be metaphysician is not that he should attack the logical positivist criterion of meaning but simply that he should make it clear what he is saying and why he is saying it. There is no *a priori* bar against his saying it at all.

II

But my aim in writing the last section was not simply that of correcting the perspective of any reader who might be still inclined to view modern British philosophy through the medium of Professor A. J. Ayer's celebrated and provocative *Language, Truth and Logic*.[19] I also wished to introduce certain ideas for brief discussion in the present section.

Mention has been made of Dr Waismann's view that every original metaphysical system embodies a vision. He seems to refer primarily to a prophetic or anticipatory vision. I do not mean to imply, for instance, that according to Dr Waismann, Descartes foresaw the work of Newton. I mean that in his view the great metaphysician had a flair for divining and expressing the really significant direction of human thought, and that Descartes' vision or picture of the comprehensibility of Nature can be seen by us as looking forward, as if it were a call or a programme, to the development of scientific thought, the most famous representative of which is Newton. But this is not a matter which I wish to discuss here. I wish instead to make some remarks about the idea of metaphysical systems as embodying visions of reality, without reference to later developments.

It is obviously true that every metaphysical system embodies a vision of reality, if we mean by 'vision' a picture or interpretation, a 'general view' as Bradley called it. And it is also obvious that when a philosopher sets out to develop his thought in systematic form he has a preliminary idea of the direction in which he is going. It would be absurd, for instance, to depict Spinoza as a kind of calculating machine. That is to say, it would be absurd to suppose that he fed himself, as it were, with certain definitions and axioms, worked out their implications in a mechanical way and discovered at the end that he was a monist. It is obvious that when he decided to present his philosophy in geometrical form he had already taken up a philosophical position. He had already conceived, in outline at least, the interpretation of reality which lent itself to presentation in such a form. He was not like a machine which has no idea where it is going but simply goes. And to this extent at least it is legitimate to make a distinction between the guiding idea (or 'vision', if one wishes to use this term) of Spinoza's system and its geometrical trappings.

But it does not follow that we are entitled to say that it is this guiding idea which alone counts and that systematic presentation can be disregarded as irrelevant. For one thing the guiding idea may become clear and articulate only through this presentation or embodiment. For another thing, even if it has definite shape beforehand, it acquires the character of a philosophy through its expression in philosophical form. A poet may have a vision of the world or of reality, but he suggests it by the use of concrete images; he is concerned with displaying it rather than with proving its truth or showing by formal argument that it is more probably true than any other theory. Of course, reference to the poet and to poetry can be misleading. For it may suggest that the distinction is one between poetry and prose. And this is not the case. A philosophy could be presented in hexameters. The distinction lies rather between the aesthetic consciousness and philosophical reflection. Both are activities of the human spirit. But they are distinguishable activities. In a given case they may be concerned in a sense with the same object but, as Hegel saw, the forms of apprehension and expression are different.

Now, the preliminary idea to which the metaphysician gives systematic conceptual expression can arise in various ways. It can arise, for instance, through advertence to some particuar aspect of empirical reality, an aspect which seems to the thinker to be all-important for an interpretation of the world. But it

may come originally from religious belief and then be rethought
philosophically, thus inspiring a metaphysical system. This is
a point of some importance. In the eyes of some people a
theistic system, for example, which is developed by a thinker
who already believes in God is necessarily bogus philosophy,
a case of mere wishful thinking. But the conclusion is by no
means necessary. If every metaphysician has some guiding idea,
some 'vision' if one wishes to use this word, and if in a given
case this guiding idea comes originally from an extra-
philosophical source, this fact is not by itself a cogent argument
against the system. The system has to be judged on its own
merits or demerits as a rational construction.

Having made this point I now wish to refer again to Mr
Strawson's distinction between descriptive and revisionary
metaphysics. We might perhaps say that the distinction lies
between the way in which we inevitably think about the world
and the way in which, according to the metaphysician, we
ought to think about it. For descriptive metaphysics is said to
be concerned with laying bare our fundamental and unchanging
conceptual structure, the concepts or categories which we
all employ whether we are reflectively conscious of employing
them or not. And revisionary metaphysics is concerned not
so much with the way in which we all actually think about the
world as with what the metaphysician thinks that reason
demands that we should think about it. Hegel, for example,
would presumably count as a revisionary metaphysician. He
did not think that all human beings actually conceive the world
in terms of the Hegelian system. But he thought that the
system answered to reason's demands. Sartre evidently does
not suppose that all men think about the world in terms of
atheistic existentialism. But he presumably thinks that they
ought to, in the sense that it is the rational way of conceiving
the world. Similarly, it is not all men who believe in God.
But the theistic metaphysician is convinced that it is at least
more reasonable to accept the existence of God than not to
accept it.

Now, according to Mr Strawson, 'revisionary metaphysics is
at the service of descriptive metaphysics'.[20] I am not quite sure
of his meaning. But he appears to mean that reflection on the
changing concepts of successive metaphysical systems can be

of use in helping to elucidate the fundamental and unchanging conceptual structure of human thought. This may very well be the case. At the same time I should not care to say that what he calls revisionary metaphysics is at the service of descriptive metaphysics. I should prefer to put things the other way round. I should prefer to say that investigation of the categories which we all employ in thinking about the world forms the basis for inquiry into the way in which we ought to conceive reality ('ought' signifying a demand of reason) over and above the way in which we inevitably conceive it.

Of course, if one accepts the Kantian revolution and looks on descriptive metaphysics, considered as an inquiry into the fundamental and unchanging conceptual structure of human thought, as the only form of metaphysics capable of providing us with knowledge, one can hardly regard what Mr Strawson calls 'revisionary metaphysics' as possessing anything more than a subordinate value. But if one regards descriptive metaphysics more from an Aristotelian point of view, namely as revealing not only the fundamental ways in which man thinks about the world but also the fundamental ontological structure of things, one can look on it as a stage in a continuous process of reflection which is carried on throughout the whole of metaphysics. And in the next section I wish to make a few remarks about this continuous movement of the mind in metaphysics as a whole.

III

It is a commonplace to say that metaphysical philosophers have concerned themselves with the problem of the Many and the One. Of course, if one puts the matter in this way, one has to show that the existence of the Many gives rise to a problem and that this problem can be solved only by reference to the One. But for the time being I content myself with saying that the movement of the mind in metaphysics is directed towards the unconditioned and ultimate reality, the Absolute. By using this term I do not intend to commit myself to monism. But if we regard the movement of the mind in metaphysics as rising from the conditioned to the unconditioned, from the finite to the infinite, the nature of the unconditioned and infinite is at first an open question, in the sense that it has yet to be determined.[21] The concept of God, however, is a determination of the nature of the ultimate reality. Hence for the moment I prefer to speak of the Absolute, provided that this word is not understood as signifying, for instance, the universe considered as a self-sufficient totality. For this concept is itself a determination of the nature of the Absolute. It is, indeed, an incorrect determination. That is to say, the claim of the world to be the Absolute is a claim which has subsequently to be exposed as bogus. But this is an irrelevant point at the moment.

What I am saying is that in my opinion the chief problem of metaphysics is the problem of the Absolute. At the close of a discussion of existentialism I wrote that 'if these final remarks give the impression that for me the problem of God is the metaphysical problem, this is a correct impression.'[22] I stand by this statement, but for reasons already indicated I prefer for the moment to speak about the problem of the Absolute. I do not, of course mean to imply that the whole of philosophy, including practical philosophy, is directly concerned with the Absolute. According to Hegel the object of philosophy is 'God and nothing but God and the unfolding of God'.[23] But for him the whole of reality is the process whereby Spirit, self-thinking thought, realises itself, coming to be explicitly what it already is implicitly. And philosophy is concerned with the essential moments of this process. Philosophy is thus always concerned with the immanent life of infinite Spirit, 'God'. But this is not the position which I wish to assert. My position is much better represented by the statement of St Thomas Aquinas that 'the whole of first philosophy (Metaphysics) is directed towards the knowledge of God as its final end.[24] That is to say, the part of metaphysics which more or less corresponds to what Mr Strawson calls 'descriptive metaphysics' is a phase in the movement of the mind towards its final goal. However, mention of Hegel is not altogether inappropriate. For though metaphysical philosophers have propounded different systems, they have all, I think, been concerned with the ultimate reality and its self-manifestation.

This movement of the mind in philosophy from multiplicity to unity has been interpreted by some critics as the expression of a misplaced craving for generality. In his so-called Blue Book, Wittgenstein found one of the sources of the philosopher's craving for generality in 'preoccupation with the method of science. I mean the method of reducing the explanation of natural phenomena to the smallest possible number of primitive natural laws. . . .'[25] Philosophers, fascinated by the method of science, tend to imitate it. And 'this tendency is the real source of metaphysics, and leads the philosopher into complete darkness'.[26] I do not think that later on Wittgenstein would have wished to lay such stress on this particular source of metaphysics. But if we take his statements as they stand, it is obvious that they are open to serious objection. We can certainly call to mind philosophers who have been influenced by this or that science. But the craving for generality in metaphysics can hardly be the result of a desire to imitate the method of science when science as we know it arose long after metaphysics. True, Wittgenstein also mentions the influence of generalisation in mathematics. And it must be admitted that mathematics exercised an influence on philosophy at a very early date. We have only to think of the Pythagoreans. But it would be very difficult to show that the movement of the mind in metaphysics towards an ultimate reality was the result of this influence. It seems to me that the so-called craving for generality in the sciences, the tendency towards unification, is a manifestation of the general movement of the theoretical reason. In metaphysics, where we are concerned primarily with existence, with the *that* of things rather than with their how,[27] this movement is directed towards an ultimate reality, an ultimate existent, rather than towards primitive 'laws'.

Reference has been made to the movement of the theoretical reason. But it is ultimately man himself, the human person, who is moved. And I should wish to connect the movement of the mind in metaphysics with the finality of the human person. However, it is more convenient to speak of the finality of the human spirit, as metaphysics is an activity of man as spiritual. We can recall the words of Spinoza. 'The love for a thing eternal and infinite alone feeds the mind with pleasure and is free from all pain. So it is much to be desired and to be sought for with all our might.'[28] I do not of course quote these words to indicate acceptance of Spinoza's idea of the relation of the finite to the infinite. I quote them as an example of the way in which at least some leading metaphysicians have connected the movement of the mind towards the Absolute with the finality of the human spirit. If I may disregard here my resolution to abstain for the time being from determining the nature of the Absolute, I should wish to assert that finite spirit has as its end a participation in the self-knowledge and self-love of infinite Spirit. True, philosophising can attain this goal only in an extremely inadequate and shadowy way. I have no desire to follow Hegel in subordinating religion to philosophy. At the same time I see in metaphysics, with all its inadequacy and shortcomings, a manifestation of the finality of the human spirit.

This is, of course, an interpretation of metaphysics, an interpretation after the fact, so to speak. In spite of my quotation from Spinoza I am not suggesting that every speculative metaphysican is first conscious of 'a love for a thing eternal and infinite' and that he then sets about rationalising his heart's desire. Metaphysics is a process of rational reflection, the point of departure of which is the finite. And if this process demands the movement of transcendence, of passing, that is to say, from the finite to the Absolute, the mind of the metaphysician may very well be impelled to perform this movement of transcendence by the shock of advertence to certain features of the finite rather than by any conscious desire for the Absolute. But this does not mean that we cannot interpret metaphysical reflection as one of the paths by which the human spirit in its odyssey can approach, though only partially and dimly, its goal. I do not regard metaphysics as a mere game, but rather as the movement of the human reason towards its end or goal. The history of metaphysical systems may seem to militate against this interpretation; but a number of philosophers have, of course, tried to do the work of the scientist as well. The rise and development of the particular sciences tend not to destroy but to purify metaphysics.

The point which I am trying to make is this. Out of the original complex of inquiries which were once grouped together under the general label of philosophy the particular sciences have gradually emerged. And the result of this development is that we are faced with a choice. On the one hand, we can try to reduce metaphysics to purely descriptive metaphysics, in the sense of an inquiry into the fundamental ways in which man actually thinks about the world. We should then be concerned, in a sense, with human concepts 'before all new discoveries and inventions'[29] provided that the word 'before' is understood in a logical and not simply and solely in a temporal sense. On the other hand, we can admit the concept of metaphysics as inquiring not only into the ways in which we actually and inevitably think about the world but also into the way in which we ought to think about it, though we do not inevitably do so. In this case, however, metaphysical thought will centre round the existence of the finite and its relation to an Absolute. The movement of transcendence will be required. For metaphysics cannot compete with science on its own ground. If it attempts to do so and does so successfully, this means that it is not metaphysics. If it is called metaphysics, this is simply a misnomer. But if it attempts to compete with science and fails to do so successfully because it is not empirical science, it makes itself ridiculous. It can be justified only if it keeps to its own ground. And the development of the particular sciences tends to the purification of metaphysics.

Obviously, when I talk about metaphysics having its own ground I am not suggesting that there is need of metaphysics because the particular sciences are defective or because we can set a limit to their advance *a priori*. Astronomy, for instance, is not defective, except in the sense that it is capable of further development. Nor can we set limits *a priori* to the possible advance of astronomy in its own field. But there are problems which the astronomer does not raise, not because astronomy is defective as astronomy but because they are simply not astronomical problems. When the logical positivist ruled out metaphysical problems as meaningless, he was in a sense drawing attention to something which is quite true, namely that the problems of metaphysics are different from the problems of the particular sciences. His way of stating the difference was exaggerated, but this does not alter the fact that he saw that there is a difference.

IV

It may be said perhaps that the distinction which I have made between metaphysics as concerned with the fundamental conceptual structure of our thinking and metaphysics as concerned with the existence of the finite and its relation to the Absolute does not really correspond with the facts of the modern situation. It narrows the field of choice too much. It is equivalent to an invitation to choose between a Kantian idea of metaphysics and a classical idea, as represented, for example, by Aquinas in the pre-Kantian era and by Schelling in the post-Kantian period. But there are other possibilities. The existentialists, for instance, approach philosophy through a consideration of man, and they raise problems which, though not problems of empirical science, are not concerned with the Absolute. Thus they raise questions about the significance of human existence and human history. Surely this is a more modern approach than the old questions about the relation of the finite to the infinite with which men such as Aquinas, Spinoza, Schelling and Hegel busied themselves.

It is true, of course, that those philosophers who are generally labelled 'existentialists', whether they like it or not, place the emphasis in their philosophies on man, especially on man as free. And those who not only start with man in his situation but also remain there do not concern themselves with the Absolute. To search for the Absolute is for Merleau-Ponty a waste of time. But to say this is not to change the fundamental problems of metaphysics; it is to exclude them. And these philosophers are phenomenologists rather than metaphysicians. But with those existentialists who go beyond man in his situation and make incursions into metaphysics the problems are not, I think, radically changed, though the approach is different and the problems are given a new dress. Karl Jaspers is notably occupied with the movement of transcendence towards the Absolute or God. Heidegger, while claiming that his approach to philosophy is new, professes to be concerned with the classical problem of 'the meaning of Being'.[30] And he informs us that 'why is there something rather than nothing?' is 'the fundamental question of metaphysics'.[31] Sartre, of course, denies the existence of God. But even for him there is an Absolute, namely massive, opaque, unintelligible being, *l'en-soi*. And he speaks of the 'metaphysical problem which might be formulated thus: why does consciousness arise from being?'[32] When the existentialist turn to metaphysics the old problems tend to recur even if they are seen in a fresh light. How indeed could it be otherwise?

As for questions about the meaning or purpose of human existence and history, the questioner is obviously not asking whether human beings have, as a matter of empirical fact, ascribed meaning or purpose to their lives and to human history in general. He may be asking whether there is a personal transcendent Being who has created man with a purpose to be achieved through history. Or he may be asking whether ultimate reality is such that the historical process is necessarily teleological in character, and, if so, what this end or telos is. In other words, if such questions are admitted and not excluded, any attempt to deal with them involves what we may call classical metaphysical problems.

These remarks should not be understood as indicating any intention on my part to minimise the importance of the approach to metaphysical problems. If there are perennial problems, in the sense of problems which perpetually tend to recur, the reason is that there is an abiding situation out of which the problems arise for the human spirit. But that this is the case needs to be shown over and over again. We cannot simply accept a set of problems from the past and take it on faith that they are problems. For a problem to have any real meaning for me I must see it arising for myself. And whatever else may be said about the existentialists, they have at least given some life and reality to philosophical problems of importance.[33]

v

In the next chapter I shall be inquiring into the conditions on the part of the subject for raising metaphysical problems, in particular the problem of the Absolute. Every question requires a questioner. And reflection on the questioner may perhaps throw some light on metaphysics. Afterwards I intend to consider the conditions on the part of the object. That is to say, what are the features of empirical reality which occasion the raising of the problem of the Absolute? We shall then be able to inquire how far, if at all, the very raising of the problem anticipates its own solution. And these reflections will, I hope, prepare the way for a more formal treatment of the movement of transcendence.

In a very real sense I have nothing new to say. And, to adopt Professor Wisdom's way of speaking, I ask myself how I can give any news when there is not any news. I can perhaps only draw attention to what is in a sense already known. Beyond that I can only perform a certain movement of reflection and reflect on this movement.

7

The self and metaphysics

I T is not necessary to inquire at present whether questions about 'the world' involve an illegitimate completion of the series of phenomena, the construction of a totality where there is no totality. We are concerned with the being of the questioner. It is obvious, I think, that the raising of such questions, whether open or not to logical objection, presupposes on the part of the questioner a certain standing back from or out of the world. That is to say, he must be able, as subject, to objectify empirical reality. In this sense (though not, of course, in the mystical sense) he must be an 'ecstatic' being.

When I say that the questioner must be subject, I do not mean simply that he must possess consciousness. He must also be capable of self-consciousness: he must be able, in some sense at least, to objectify himself. For the reality which is objectified includes, of course, the questioner. He must therefore be able to stand back, as it were, from himself.

In part, therefore, I belong as object to my world. I can, of coarse, be an object for other people. But I can also be object for myself. My attention is first of all directed to the external. But it can be reflected on to myself. I can, as Hume puts it, enter into myself. And what do I then find? Let us recall Hume's often quoted and by now rather hackneyed words:

> For my part, when I enter most intimately into what I call myself, I always stumble on some particular perception or other, of heat or cold, light or shade, love or hatred, pain or pleasure. I never can catch myself at any time without a perception, and never can observe anything but the perception.[1]

Obviously, what Hume says is true up to a point. If I enter into myself and observe the furniture of the mind, I see successive, if related, psychical phenomena. I do not see myself as a distinct item of furniture alongside successive thoughts, desires, images and so on. Empirical psychology does not discover a naked self along with the other psychical phenomena it observes. I cannot sensibly say: 'I perceive a thought, a desire, an image and a self.' And still less, of course, does a behaviouristically orientated psychology discover a naked self.

Would it be reasonable to speak of one or more of these psychical items, the so-called contents or furniture of the mind, as raising metaphysical problems? Hardly, I think. A metaphysical problem, as object of my reflective consideration, is itself one of the contents of my mind. And it is I who raise it and consider it. This I, this self, cannot be simply identified with the objects of introspection, with one or more discrete psychical phenomena and to attempt this identification or reduction is to forget the necessary condition of there being any such phenomena.

One can indeed understand how Hume came to suggest that the self is nothing but the succession of psychical phenomena. It was the result of an attempt, in the interests of developing a science of man, to extend to the analysis of the self an experimental method which Hume believed to have proved its fruitfulness in the field of natural science. There is, of course, no valid objection to the development of empirical psychology. The point is, however, that it cannot, whether in its older or newer forms, provide an adequate account of the self.

To do him justice, Hume was conscious of the unsatisfactory character of his analysis of the self, and he admitted as much in explicit terms, pleading 'the privilege of a sceptic'.[2] But some of his successors appear to have no such scruples. Thus we are told by some modern empiricists that the mind is a logical construction analysable into psychical phenomena or events.[3] They appear to think that the truth of this contention should be evident to anyone who is not a benighted metaphysician or a prejudiced theologian. But they would do well to recall Bradley's apt remark: 'Mr Bain collects that the mind is a collection. Has he ever thought who collects Mr Bain?'[4] To the empiricist such remarks may seem to be cheap gibes of no value. They are nothing of the kind.

But we have been using rather unfortunate language. That is to say, in denying that the self can be identified with or reduced to the succession of psychical phenomena, the furniture or contents of the mind, we may seem to imply that the self is something over against a number of objects which it observes from without, even though they are somehow located within it. And this spatial language is unfortunate, though it is difficult to avoid it. Obviously, I am aware not merely of a thought or of a desire but of *my* thought or of *my* desire: I am aware of certain psychical phenomena as mine. Preferably, I am conscious of myself thinking or of myself desiring. By reflection I objectify myself in a certain phase of activity. Of course, the forms of language do sometimes seem to imply the furniture idea. We can speak, for instance, of ideas coming into the mind, of my having had the intention of going somewhere, and so on. And a reflective analysis of the variety of expressions which are employed in this connection in ordinary language would be doubtless worth while. But this does not alter the fact that I am now conscious of myself thinking rather than of thoughts as foreign bodies located in my mind, even though I can, as it were, detach them and talk about them.

But can I fully objectify myself? When I enter into myself, as Hume puts it, I do not perceive a self as an additional item to the other items which form the mind's so-called contents. But it is I who enter into myself; it is I who am the active subject of introspection. In fact there could be no introspection, no self-objectification, without the I-subject. The I-subject is a necessary condition for there being a me-object. And can this I-subject be objectified? It is related that Fichte invited his students to think the wall. They thought it. He then invited them to think him who thought the wall. Obviously, one could proceed indefinitely along this path. We could try to think him who thought him who thought the wall, and so on without end. We might raise the question therefore whether in each stage of reflection there is not an I-subject, a transcendental ego, which eludes all objectification.

In one sense at any rate it is true to say that the I-subject cannot be objectified. If objectification is taken to mean reduction to the status of object-for-a-subject, it is obvious that the subject, considered precisely as such, cannot be objectified. Of course, we then come perilously near to making the whole question a purely linguistic matter. In an epistemological context the words 'subject' and 'object' have distinct, though correlative, meanings. And it thus follows necessarily, by definition that is to say, that the subject, considered as such, cannot properly be spoken of as object. But it is not simply a matter of language. The fact remains that the human self is not perfectly self-luminous. I do not enjoy a self-intuition in which there is no distinction between subject and object. And in this sense at least there is a meta-phenomenal self.

But by talking about the meta-phenomenal self I in some sense objectify it. If I think and speak about the meta-phenomenal self as the principle of the unity of consciousness and as the necessary condition of all objectification, I to this extent objectify it. For it becomes that about which I think and speak. And I may thus appear to be involved in a contradiction. On the one hand, I say that there is a meta-phenomenal and unobjectifiable self. On the other hand, I cannot say this without objectifying it. But when I say that there is a meta-phenomenal and unobjectifiable self, I mean that there is a self which is the necessary condition for there being any 'objects' and which is not itself one of them. And when I think and speak about it, I think and speak about it precisely as this unobjectifiable condition. By speaking about it I tend to reduce it to an object. But my purpose in so speaking is to draw attention to the unobjectifiable condition of this objectification. In a real sense I am trying to say what cannot be said. But it can be shown. And, if we prescind from Fichte's idealism, we can perhaps say that this is what he was trying to do. It is not much help to observe that no amount of peering about will discover Fichte's pure or transcendental ego. For this was precisely Fichte's point.

How, then, can we be justified in speaking about a meta-phenomenal self at all? Is it supposed to be an inferred occult entity? No, for it manifests itself in its activity—for example, in its activity of objectification. Attention is directed first to the external, though even here I am concomitantly aware of my externally directed acts as mine. But I can also reflect on my attention to myself. And though I cannot set myself as subject over against myself and though I am not perfectly self-luminous or self-transparent, I can be aware of myself as a meta-phenomenal self in and through my objectifying activity. We do not infer the meta-phenomenal self as an occult, unmanifested entity; by reflection we become aware of it as an active, manifested principle, though this principle in itself cannot be reduced to one of its own direct objects.

It is in virtue of this meta-phenomenal self that man is capable of standing back from out of the world and raising metaphysical problems. The matter can be expressed in another way by saying that man is capable of metaphysics in so far as he is spirit. Metaphysics is a spiritual activity; it reveals the spiritual nature of the questioner. By saying this I do not intend to imply, of course, that metaphysical reflection is the only spiritual activity of man. Science, artistic creation and religious experience are also spiritual activities. Nor do I intend to imply that metaphysics is the most important spiritual activity of man. I certainly do not wish to follow Hegel in assigning the supreme expression of spirit to philosophy. But we are concerned here with metaphysics, and I cannot undertake to discuss the whole range of man's spiritual activity.

There is, I think, a close connection between man's spiritual nature and what in the last chapter I called the movement of transcendence in metaphysics. As spirit, man transcends the material world, and his end lies outside it. In the last chapter I advanced the thesis that this end is a participation in the self-knowledge and self-love of infinite Spirit. And the movement of transcendence towards the Absolute is to be interpreted in the light of the finality of finite spirit. If I make these remarks in a dogmatic manner, the reason is that I am concerned in this paragraph simply with clarifying my position by linking the foregoing reflection about the self with the thesis which was advanced at an earlier stage in the discussion as a whole.

II

Wittgenstein asks, 'Where in the world is a metaphysical subject to be noted?'.[5] And there is a sense in which it is correct to answer 'Nowhere'. That is to say, if by the world we mean all that is correlative as object to the subject, the subject clearly cannot be noted in the world. We might then feel inclined to say with Wittgenstein that 'the subject does not belong to the world but it is a limit of the world'.[6] At the same time it would be obviously absurd to depict man as being simply a metaphysical subject in an epistemological sense. In the previous section I referred to Bradley's remark about Bain. But elsewhere Bradley pertinently alludes to the reduction of the self to a 'wretched fraction and poor atom', and he asks, 'Do you mean to tell me that this bare remnant is really the self? The supposition is preposterous, and the question needs no answer.'[7] Bradley is talking primarily about the search for an abiding and unchanging self, but his question is applicable to any identification of man with a metaphysical subject or transcendental ego.

We can put the matter in this way. Man is spirit, but he is certainly not pure spirit. He is not a spirit which happens to have a body as a possession or instrument. His body belongs to himself in the wider sense of the word 'self'. If I strike someone's body, I do not simply strike something which he has or owns; I strike him. Man is essentially embodied or incarnate spirit. And his psychical life is naturally dependent in many ways on his presence in the world in virtue of his embodied or incarnate condition.[8]

If, therefore, we say that man stands out from the physical cosmos, from Nature, we must also say that he is in it. If we wish to say that man transcends the world, we must also say, paradoxically, that he transcends it as a being in the world. He is an 'ecstatic' being as a being in the world, and he is a being in the world as an 'ecstatic' being. Such paradoxes serve to draw attention to man's peculiar nature as embodied or incarnate spirit.

But when in the present context we speak of man as a being in the world, we do not mean only that he is corporally present in the world. We mean also that he is involved therein. Man cannot live without acting, and he acts in and through the world. This is obviously true on the level of the satisfaction of man's bodily needs as a physical organism. But it is also true on other levels. For instance, as spirit man has a moral vocation; he acts in accordance with ideals of some sort or another. But

J

this moral vocation has to be fulfilled in and through action in the world. Further, even though man as spirit may have, and in my opinion certainly has, a final end which transcends the world, he can tend towards this end only through self-commitment within the world. The world is the arena or field in which his vocation is or is not fulfilled. As a moral agent man is involved in the world.

Now, man's condition of being involved as actor in the world is, I think, one of the springs of metaphysical questioning. It is not, of course, acting as such which originates metaphysical problems. A man can absorb himself, for instance, in the actions which lead to the satisfaction of his physical needs and desires and seek only that degree of understanding which is required for this purpose. This degree is obviously a variable factor. But, whatever the degree, on this level metaphysical problems do not arise. For the mind is used simply as an instrument for the satisfaction of determinate physical needs and desires. But man is capable of objectifying to himself the whole vista, as it were, of his life of free choice and action from birth to death, and he can ask whether this active flight from birth to death is simply something which happens or whether it has a significance beyond the mere fact that it happens. The fact that he can raise such a question depends on his having the character of what I have called standing out from the world. He can raise it because he is an ecstatic being, spirit. But he is impelled to raise the question by advertence to his being involved as actor in a world which does not bear the answer clearly on its face in such a way that no question can arise.

The use of such terms as 'ecstatic being' and 'objectification' may give the impression that we are treating of a matter which is far removed from ordinary experience. But it is really quite simple. Albert Camus speaks of the man who goes habitually through his ordinary routine of life and then one day suddenly asks the question 'Why?' He asks, that is to say, what is the point of it all. He is obviously not asking what is the point of his going to work every weekday, if by 'the point' we mean the purpose served within the framework of his daily life. He knows very well the answer to this question. He is asking a question about the 'ultimate' significance of his life and existence as a whole. There may be logical difficulties which can be raised in regard to such a question. And it can hardly be said to be a simple matter to deal with these difficulties. At the same time the situation described by Camus is not so exceptional or so unrelated to ordinary experience that non-philosophers are incapable of understanding what he is talking about.

I have spoken of a standing back from or out of the stream of life, thus employing the analogy of a man immersed in a stream who gets his head above the water and can survey the scene though he is at the same time travelling with the current. And the analogy may have its uses. But, for it to be applicable, the term 'stream of life' has to be understood in a very restricted sense. For metaphysical reflection is itself a form of life. (So, of course, is science.) Metaphysical reflection is one of the forms which the life of the spirit can take in its movement towards its goal. And to oppose metaphysics to life is a mistake, unless, as I have indicated, the word 'life' is understood in a narrow sense.

To return to the question about the significance of human existence or of human history. As was remarked in the previous chapter such questions necessarily involve questions about God or about the nature of ultimate reality. But though such questions involve reference to God or to ultimate reality, they are asked about human existence or about human history. Similarly, a question such as 'Why is there something rather than nothing?' concerns the 'something', the empirically existent, even though it is a metaphysical question. In other words, the approach to metaphysics and the form of the questions is determined by man's being in the world as involved therein.

The matter can be summed up in this way. That man can raise metaphysical questions or problems is due to his capacity to stand back from or out of the world. It is rooted in his nature as spirit, as an 'ecstatic' being. But that he raises metaphysical questions which have the empirically given as their point of departure is due to his involvement in the world, to his nature as embodied or incarnate spirit. To ask the questions which are in fact asked, the questioner must have a complex nature. He must transcend the physical cosmos as a being in the world, and he must be involved in the physical cosmos as a being which at the same time transcends it. The movement of transcendence towards the Absolute, which is characteristic of metaphysical speculation, is ultimately rooted in the finality of finite spirit. But that it is a movement of transcending empirical reality as a point of departure is due to the 'involved' nature of the human spirit.

III

I have proposed the thesis that the human spirit is teleologically orientated towards a participation in the self-knowledge and self-love of infinite Spirit. But I have also maintained that inasmuch as man is a being in the world and involved therein, the movement towards the Absolute is a movement of transcendence, a movement by way of reflection on empirical reality. I have also allowed that it is possible for a man to absorb himself in a level of life at which metaphysical problems have little or no meaning for him. The question therefore arises, what are the features of empirical reality which occasion the movement of transcendence? If the movement demands conditions on the part of the subject, the questioner, does it not also demand conditions on the part of the object, that is, of the objective point of departure, the empirically given?

I have little doubt that the features of things which principally impel the mind to raise the problem of the Absolute are those features which I propose to call the more obvious or evident manifestations of contingency. It may be objected that the word 'contingent' should be reserved for propositions and not applied to things. But it will hardly be denied, I think, that mutability, insecurity and instability are features of at least many things. And these are what I mean by the more obvious manifestations of contingency. So I do not think that discussion of the use of the word 'contingent' need detain us, not at least at this stage of our reflections.

These features are obviously found in many things external to man, in the flowers of the field for example. They are found also in man himself. And the most obvious example is perhaps death. Man finds himself in the world without any originating choice on his part. We can perfectly well give a cash-value to Heidegger's term, *Die Geworfenheit des Daseins*, man's 'thrownness' or 'projection' into the world. And mortality attends upon him from the start. There is no need to elaborate this theme.

It may be as well to draw attention to the fact that I have spoken of the more evident manifestations of contingency as features which are found in at least many things, including man himself. I have not spoken of all things. Still less have I asserted that the world is a contingent thing. For the moment my point is simply that it is certain features, which are found in many things, which principally occasion the movement of the mind towards the Absolute. It is quite possible for the mind to proceed from these features as found in many things to an absolutisation of the world or the universe—to the picture, that is to say, of the world as a kind of absolute entity which contains a multiplicity of existentially unstable things. And I hope to return later to this theme of the pseudo-Absolute, the candidate for the rank of Absolute whose claims have to be unmasked. For the time being I leave this matter aside. It is sufficient to note that we can observe in at least many things those features which I have called the more obvious or evident manifestations of contingency.

Now, I have spoken of such features as impelling the mind to raise the problem of the Absolute. But this is obviously inaccurate. It is the mind's advertence to these features as manifestations of a radical instability and insecurity on the plane of existence which leads it to raise this problem. What I mean by advertence in this context can be illustrated by a simple example. Not much experience is required to be aware of the empirical fact that human beings die. And every normal man is aware that his own mortality is included in this general proposition. But it does not necessarily follow that every man actually adverts to the fact of human mortality in general, and of his own in particular, as a manifestation of a radical existential instability, of contingency. We may read in the paper that some prominent figure, well advanced in years, has died. We register the fact as an item of information and turn to the Sports page. Or we can look on dying from the point of view of the empirical scientist. In neither case does one perform what I call the act of adverting to death as a manifestation of existential contingency.

The choice of death as an example to illustrate the difference between being aware of an empirical fact and adverting to it as a manifestation of existential contingency may indeed give an unfortunate impression. Lucretius maintained, and not without some reason, that it is not so much death by itself which gives reasonable ground for fear as belief in an afterlife in which divine sanctions are inflicted. However, it is true that advertence to one's own inevitable death is to many people an unpleasing thought which may even cause horror and dread or *Angst*. Hence they normally tend to shun the thought. And it may thus appear that my mention of advertence to death is tantamount to an implicit admission that metaphysical questions are the expression of emotive states. In other words, the difference between advertence and non-advertence, it may be said, is equivalent to the difference between the presence and absence of an emotive attitude towards the empirical facts. For I have admitted that all normal men are aware of human mortality. If therefore we presuppose this awareness, what remains to constitute 'advertence' except an emotive reaction produced by dwelling on the facts when seen in a certain light?

The answer can be given that by advertence in this context is meant advertence to the facts precisely as manifestations of existential contingency, of instability and lack of self-sufficiency in the existential order. And this is an intellectual act which should not be confused with the emotional or affective response which it may possibly, but not necessarily, evoke. Centuries ago, Aristotle drew attention to the need of distinguishing between an activity and the pleasure which accompanies it. And an analogous distinction must be made in the present context. To advert to my mortality for instance, is to advert to it as a manifestation of my existential contingency and lack of self-sufficiency. My presence in this world is not a necessary presence, except, of course, in the sense that I cannot be absent while I am present. And to advert to this is to advert to a truth. It is an intellectual act which may or may not evoke a particular emotional reaction.

Of course, I am quite prepared to admit that emotive states may play a part in impelling a man to raise metaphysical problems when these are raised as matters of personal concern and importance. They may, for instance, play a part in helping to liberate man from absorption in or exclusive riveting of his attention on his physical needs and from exclusive preoccupation with his social cares. It is not simply a question of heightened emotive attitudes, such as dread, *Angst* or *angoisse*. 'Wonder' has often been mentioned as the basis of metaphysical reflection. But cannot wonder be called an emotive state? Certainly, it is an emotive response following an intellectual act of advertence. For one presumably wonders at something which one has noted, recognised or adverted to. But this is just my point, namely that we must distinguish between the intellectual act of advertence and the emotive state or response which it may evoke. Insistence on this distinction entails rejection of the view that metaphysical problems are simply the expression of emotion. But it does not entail refusal to admit that emotive overtones can play in impelling a man to raise such problems as matters of personal concern and importance. After all, man, the questioner, is not simply a desiccated reason.

The view that metaphysical problems are the expression of feeling can indeed be made very plausible. It may be said, for instance, that mutability, taken as a fact, gives rise to no problems. For what can a material thing, or indeed any finite thing be but mutable in some way? If, however, one fixes one's attention on the changing character of things, a general sense of mutability, a general feeling of changeability and transitoriness may be produced. Clear expressions of this general feeling or sense can be found in some of the poets. Rilke's poem on autumn might perhaps be cited as an example. The falling of the leaves is the image which evokes the feeling of general instability and transitoriness.

Wir alle fallen. Diese Hand da fällt.
Und sieh dir andere an: es ist in allen.

This general feeling of mutability and contingency, it might be argued, is one of the most powerful sources of the search for the Absolute.

Now, I certainly do not wish to deny the possibility of what has been described in the last paragraph as a general sense or feeling of mutability and transitoriness. Nor do I wish to deny that it may have played a part in stimulating the search for the Absolute. No doubt it has. But what is a general feeling of mutability? If it means a kind of global advertence to the mutability of very many things, this is an intellectual act. It may indeed evoke some emotive response. It might evoke, for example, a feeling of melancholy. But a global advertence to the mutability of very many things is not itself a feeling or emotive state.

Of course, what the critic probably wishes to suggest is that advertence to the mutability or to the existential instability of many things can produce a feeling or impression of the world as a limited and contingent totality or whole, and that this feeling or impression is the source of the search for the Absolute. In other words, the search for the Absolute is the fruit of what Wittgenstein calls 'the mystical feeling'.[9] But I question this interpretation. As I have already indicated, it is possible for the mind to move from a global advertence to the mutability or to the existential instability of many things, to the idea of the world or universe as an infinite Absolute. Initially, that is to say, the movement of transcendence is not necessarily a transcendence of the idea of the world or universe. For it is possible to see the finite against the background, as it were, of a world or universe considered as an infinite Absolute. This is possible on the level of systematic metaphysics. We find it, for instance in Spinoza's doctrine of infinite Substance. And it is possible too on the level of what can be called spontaneous metaphysics. This is indeed a pseudo-Absolute. But I do not wish to discuss this matter now. The point for the moment is that in this movement of the mind nothing is asserted about the contingency of the world or universe.

The so-called global sense of mutability, of transitoriness and of lack of existential self-sufficiency therefore is not, in my opinion, equivalent to a feeling or impression of the world or universe as a limited and contingent totality. Rather is it equivalent to (or, if taken as a feeling, the emotive response to) an implicit recognition of the contingency of the finite as such without, however, any accompanying judgement that the world or universe is finite and contingent. I say 'an implicit recognition', because what is actually adverted to, at the level of reflection which I have in mind, is the manifestation of contingency in many things. Hence I should say that the fundamental condition on the part of the object for the movement of transcendence, for the raising of the problem of the Absolute, is the existence of at least one finite thing, manifesting its contingency to the subject. As far as the initial movement of the mind is concerned, it may terminate in a vaguely conceived and erroneous idea of the Absolute. But the nature of the point of departure is, I think, fairly clear.

IV

But we are by no means out of the wood yet. And in this section I wish to put into the mouth of a hypothetical critic a line of objection which I shall be discussing in the next chapter. In the remaining paragraphs of this chapter it will be the critic who is speaking.

'You have spoken as though the mutability and existential instability of finite things gave rise to a metaphysical problem. But why do you think this? If you wished to argue that because one finite thing comes into existence in dependence on other finite things, the whole series of finite things must be existentially dependent on something which is not itself finite, I should know what you were talking about, though I should maintain that you were involved in logical fallacies. But so far at least you have tried to keep the world as a totality out of the discussion. You appear to believe that the existence of any finite things is sufficient to warrant what you call the movement of transcendence. But why do you believe it?

'I think that I can answer this question for you. Like other speculative metaphysicians you are looking for a One, an unconditioned and ultimate reality, a divine infinite. With Spinoza you feel that only 'a thing eternal and infinite' can satisfy your desire. You do not find it, needless to say, among finite things, the things with which we become acquainted through experience. You are therefore impelled by dissatisfaction with the finite to proceed further to perform what you call the movement of transcendence. But why should one be dissatisfied with the characteristics of the finite? The finite cannot be other than it is. The dissatisfaction makes sense only in virtue of a comparison of the finite with an ideal, the existence of which, as term of a desire, is presupposed. You assume that there must be an Absolute. And this assumption is the expression of the heart's desire.

'As you are well aware, Wittgenstein asserted that "not *how* the world is, is the mystical, but *that* it is".[10] And frankly, I think that your line of thought moves within the field of mysticism. Of course, if you are prepared to admit this, it would be inappropriate for me to press objections about want of clarity and logical rigour. For one cannot justifiably expect these qualities in the field of the mystical. But the trouble with metaphysicians is that they try to have things both ways by giving logical philosophical form to a content which does not lend itself to this form. They claim to be following where reason leads when in reality they are following the heart's desire. Mysticism may have its place in life. At least it is irrelevant to my purpose to argue that it has not. But mystical reflections should not masquerade as philosophical arguments.

'Your idea of the Absolute doubtless differs from that of Bradley. But I imagine your attitude is pretty well represented by the following quotation from that philosopher. "The want of an object, and, still more, the search for an object, imply in a certain sense the knowledge of that object. If a man supposed that he could never tell when possession is or is not gained, he surely never would pursue. In and by the pursuit he commits himself to the opposite assumption, and that assumption must rest on a possession which to some extent and in some sense is there."[11] Advertence to those features of the finite which you have called manifestations of contingency shows that the finite is not what you are seeking. Well and good, but does it follow that the mind is logically justified in performing the movement of transcendence and asserting the existence of that which you seek? Your movement of transcendence seems to me to resemble closely Karl Jaspers' "philosophical faith". It seems to me to be the expression of a desire, the causes of which provide matter of inquiry for the psychologist rather than for the philosopher. If you are willing to admit this, we can let the matter rest. But if you reject my interpretation of your procedure, perhaps you would care to make some comments on it in your next chapter.'

8
The metaphysics of the Absolute and desire

I N the final section of my last chapter I put into the mouth of an imagined critic some objections against my line of thought. The critic's main contention was that the primary and fundamental element in metaphysics as I conceive it is the desire for the Absolute, in the sense of an infinite and un-conditioned reality. What I have called the movement of transcendence is not a movement of the mind which is required in order to solve any definable problem or to answer any genuine question which arises out of the existence of the finite. Rather is it the expression of the heart's desire which fails to find satisfaction in the finite. Thus to affirm the Absolute is not to explain anything which stands in need of explanation; it is to affirm one's faith in a reality the existence of which is for some reason desired. And arguments to prove the existence and exhibit the nature of the Absolute are so many attempts to give rational form to a belief which is ultimately based on desire and not on rational grounds. In other words, the metaphysician is impelled by a deep-seated urge or tendency which is more fundamental than any arguments that he may adduce in support of his beliefs. The desire for the Absolute may some-times betray itself in explicit statements, as we have seen with Spinoza and Bradley, but it tends to be concealed behind a mass of argumentation which in actual fact plays a quite subordinate role.

It scarcely needs saying, I think, that the imagined critic was in fact myself. The criticism was self-criticism: it was a challenge to myself to clarify my position. It is, therefore, obvious that my alter ego must have felt that there was some truth in the objections. Hence what is required is a clarifying meditation on my position rather than an attempt to dispose summarily of the critic as a tiresome fellow whose point of view is unworthy of serious consideration. His objections are, however, so wide-ranging that they cannot be dealt with all at once. Further, in view of the fact that I have not yet developed my position in a systematic manner it would be inappropriate to confine myself to answering, or attempting to answer, objections against it. What I propose to do in this and succeeding chapters is to develop my position in the light of my alter ego's criticism. And I hope that in this way it will become apparent to what extent the criticism is relevant to my idea of metaphysics.

To begin with, I intend to discuss the role of desire in metaphysics as I conceive it. There appears indeed to be a certain ambiguity in the critic's remarks on this subject. For though we may be accustomed to speak of unconscious desires, the word 'desire', when used without this qualification, seems to refer ordinarily to a conscious process, whereas terms such as 'urge', 'drive' and so on suggest something which lies beneath the threshold of consciousness. And for this reason I propose to ask two questions. First, what part does conscious desire play in metaphysics as I conceive it? Secondly, does my account of metaphysics imply that it is the rationalised expression of some unconscious desire, urge or drive? I dare say that these questions cannot be treated in complete separation from one another. But I shall try at any rate to make a rough division, even if I am not entirely successful.

II

In the first place there is an obvious sense in which desire is certainly a fundamental element in metaphysics as in any other branch of inquiry. In a paper entitled 'The Function of Metaphysics' I wrote in this way: 'Philosophy is rooted in the desire to understand the world, in the desire to find an intelligible pattern in events and to answer problems which occur to the mind in connection with the world.'[1] 'In its origins metaphysics arises simply out of a natural desire to understand the world or the historical situation.'[2] My motive at the time in making such statements was to point out that discussion of the logical status of metaphysical questions follows the raising of such questions, and that they were raised in the first place simply because the people who did so wished to understand something. Even if we were to go on to assert that the questions were only pseudo-questions from the logical point of view, the fact would remain that the conscious desire of those who raised them was to understand the world, the term 'world' being used in a sense which does not exclude the questioner. My motive in repeating the point here is to draw attention to the fact that there is nothing to be ashamed of in admitting that desire is a fundamental element in metaphysics. Without the desire to understand, no science would have arisen or developed. And nobody would dream of condemning science on this ground.

My alter ego's obvious retort to this is that nobody dreams of condemning metaphysics on the ground that it is the fruit of a desire to understand the world. For the matter of that it is not primarily a question of 'condemning' metaphysics. Some metaphysicians, especially those who have confined themselves to what Mr Strawson calls 'descriptive metaphysics', may have been motivated simply by the desire to understand. But this is not the point at issue. The question at issue is whether my idea of metaphysics, as outlined in these articles, does not imply that it is the rationalised expression of a particular desire, the desire for the Absolute. Is not the motive which inspires the whole process of argumentation in metaphysics as I conceive it the desire to prove the truth of a particular conclusion when its truth has already been assumed because the philosopher wishes it to be true? If this is indeed the case, it can hardly be claimed that the metaphysician, as I depict him, is motivated by an unprejudiced desire to understand the world.

It is true, of course, that no sane man would condemn metaphysics on the ground that it is the fruit of a desire to understand the world. Some people maintain that the world gives rise to no problems the solution of which requires the development of a metaphysics. But the desire to understand is not itself regarded as a reason for questioning the value of metaphysics, still less as a ground for outright condemnation. At the same time the mere mention of the word 'desire' in connection with metaphysical reflection is sufficient to render the latter suspect for some minds. And it is as well to dissipate this initial prejudice by calling attention to the fact, even if it is an obvious fact, that in all scientific inquiry desire is a fundamental element. However, it is also true that my critic's objections concern a particular desire, the desire for the Absolute. And I wish to inquire briefly how far, if at all, my idea of metaphysics implies that the metaphysician is impelled by a conscious desire to prove the truth of a preconceived belief in the Absolute.

III

If we say that the finite spirit is orientated towards the Absolute in the sense, for instance, that the potentialities of spirit are not completely actualised by the finite, that spirit involves a capacity for the infinite, and if we say that metaphysics is a manifestation of this capacity and one of the ways in which spirit can approach its goal, we are not saying that every human being consciously desires the Absolute. We are not committed to denying what appears to be the evident empirical fact that it is by no means all men who desire the Absolute, when the word 'desire' is taken in its ordinary sense. We are stating something about the nature of finite spirit rather than something about its conscious desires. We can indeed go on to interpret the restless striving of man in his intellectual and volitional aspects as a striving informed by the finality of finite spirit. But this interpretation does not commit us to maintaining that every man consciously apprehends the goal of his striving and desires it.

At the same time it can obviously be objected that we are concerned here with the metaphysician, not with every human being. And have I not asserted in chapter 6 that when a philosopher sets out to develop his thought in systematic form he has a preliminary idea of the direction in which he is going, a preliminary guiding idea or general view of reality? If, therefore, metaphysics, as I conceive it, is concerned with the Absolute, am I not committed to saying that the metaphysician has a preliminary idea of the Absolute? And must I not then admit that the systematic development of the metaphysician's thought constitutes an attempt to establish the truth of a preconceived idea? It is not, of course, preconceived in the sense of being an innate idea. But in relation to the system with its argumentation, the idea is preconceived. In fact it is not simply a case of a preconceived idea; the idea forms part of a presupposed belief. And in this sense we can say that the elaboration and formal development of the metaphysician's thought is informed by the desire to establish the truth of a presupposed belief.

This is a difficult matter to deal with. For though there are doubtless family likenesses between metaphysicians, we can hardly say that all metaphysicians are cast in the same mould or that they all approach the development of their systems in precisely the same way. We have to take account of differences. It is indeed undeniable that some philosophers have begun with a determinate idea of the Absolute and with a firm belief in its validity. It is an obvious historical fact that with Aquinas, for instance, religious belief in God preceded philosophical reflection on the evidence presented by the world for God's existence. But in other cases the preliminary determinate idea, when there is one, may be derived not so much from any definite religious creed as from what we might be tempted, in more relaxed moments, to call an intuitive view of reality. I say 'in more relaxed moments' because to speak of intuition in this context is, I think, a lazy way of talking. What we are faced with is really a preliminary philosophical canter, a swift inference suggested by various factors and taking on the appearance of an intuition when it is compared with a systematically developed philosophy. In this case the pre-liminary idea does not lie outside philosophy. I did indeed remark earlier (p. 102) that the philosopher's vision or guiding idea 'acquires the character of a philosophy through its expression in philosophical form'. And if one restricts the application of the term 'philosophy' to the systematic presen-tation of a philosopher's thought, we shall have to say that any preliminary guiding ideas which he may have had did not constitute philosophy until they entered into and formed part of this systematic presentation. But this is a rather narrow use of the term 'philosophy'. And in any case when I spoke of the philosopher's preliminary vision or guiding idea as acquiring the character of a philosophy through its expression in philosophical form, I was thinking primarily of more or less vague and inarticulate ideas, whereas we are concerned here with determinate preliminary ideas. And the formation of these determinate ideas can reasonably be regarded, as I have said above, as a preliminary philosophical canter.

In any case it is by no means inevitable that the philosopher should be resolved at all costs to prove the validity of his preliminary determinate vision or guiding idea. For he might choose to regard it as a hypothesis. This will indeed hardly be the case when there is question of a preceding and firmly held religious belief. But it may very well apply in other instances. And even in the case of a preceding and firmly held religious belief it does not follow that the philosopher who starts with this belief is determined to prove its truth at all costs. If it is a belief which he judges for some reason to fall within the possible scope of philosophy, he may very well desire to find a cogent philosophical proof of its truth. But it is open to him to say that he has found no argument which seems to him convincing. The presence of an initial desire to prove does not entail subsequent intellectual dishonesty.

But it is not necessary that the philosopher who arrives at a theory of the Absolute should have a preliminary determinate idea of it, the validity of which he wishes to establish if possible. One can imagine, for example, a philosopher forming a vague preliminary notion of degrees of reality, or of the analogy of being. He might wish to say, for instance, that the dream is 'less real' than the dreamer. Some might perhaps comment that the dream is just as real as the dreamer, for it is a real dream. Or they might wish to say that the philosopher's perplexity is in principle curable through its being pointed out to him that the reality is a person dreaming. But let us pass over this discussion and assume that a philosopher has formed a perhaps rather vague notion of degrees of reality. He might then set out to discover ultimate reality or being in the sense of that thing or those things of which we can say in the primary sense that it or they exist. The notion of ultimate reality or being then forms for him a guiding idea. But it need not be the idea of an ultimate reality transcending the phenomenal world, as far as the philosopher's initial presuppositions are concerned. One cannot indeed deny the possibility of a philosopher setting out to search for an ultimate reality which is not identifiable with the phenomenal world. But in this case we could probably find in his preliminary philosophical canter an adumbration of his reasons for conceiving ultimate reality in this way. In any case my point is that the attempt to give a content to the guiding idea of ultimate reality or being does not necessarily presuppose any determinate idea of the Absolute, the validity of which the philosopher is set on establishing by formal argumentation. Of course, the term 'ultimate reality' tends to suggest to us the notion of a reality behind, so to speak, the empirical world. But as far as a philosopher's necessary presuppositions are concerned, ultimate reality or being might turn out to be the universe itself.

I do not think, therefore, that I am committed to saying that the metaphysician's reflection is governed by a conscious desire to establish the truth of a preconceived determinate belief in the Absolute. I have indeed admitted that certain metaphysicians had pre-existing beliefs derived from extra-philosophical sources. But this is to admit a biographical fact rather than to make a statement about what is necessarily involved by metaphysics. If we leave such cases out of account, any so-called preconceived idea is, I think, the result of a preliminary philosophical canter. And this really belongs to philosophy itself. That is to say, the formation of a preliminary idea, whether more or less determinate, and its subsequent systematic articulation form one total process of philosophical reflection. It is perhaps true that we do not generally speak of those as philosophers who get as far as a general vision of reality but who never give to the vision anything which could reasonably be called a systematic expression. At the same time we could perfectly well speak of them as philosophers if we wished to do so, provided that their vision of reality had not been accepted simply on authority.

IV

To turn now to the question of a drive or urge or unconscious desire behind metaphysics. In the paper on 'The Function of Metaphysics' to which I have already alluded I wrote as follows: 'We are all familiar with children asking for explan-

K

ations without any other obvious motive than that of resolving
some perplexity, solving some difficulty or understanding some
event or set of events: and I suggest that philosophy, as far
as its original motive is concerned, is inspired by the same sort
of desire which is observable in children.'[3] But I also allowed
for the possibility of discussing 'whether the desire to understand
ought to be interpreted or analysed in terms of another drive
or other drives'.[4] And it is arguable that by describing metaphysics as a manifestation of the finite spirit's orientation to
the Absolute I have based it in some sense on a drive. True,
those who maintain that the type of metaphysics which
culminates in the idea of the Absolute is in fact grounded on
a drive or urge of some sort would doubtless also maintain that
it pertains to the psychologists to determine the nature of the
drive. They might point out that I myself referred to 'these
psychological questions'.[5] And they would probably say that I
have no business to explain metaphysics in terms of a particular
metaphysical theory which is itself part of the *explicandum*, of
what has to be explained. At the same time they would probably
also claim that by interpreting metaphysics in terms of the
finality of finite spirit I am admitting, in my own misguided
way, that metaphysics is the rationalised expression of a drive.

Now, we might well ask with what right a philosopher claims
that metaphysics is the expression of an unconscious desire or
urge or drive if at the same time he disclaims any competence
to determine the nature of the drive.[6] How does he know that
metaphysics is the expression of a drive? I suppose that the
situation is more or less this: those who insist that behind
metaphysical philosophy there is some powerful drive, the
nature of which they leave to the psychologists to determine,
are often to be found among those who are sceptical of metaphysical arguments, at least in so far as such arguments are
claimed to be logical proofs, and who do not regard metaphysics as a possible source of knowledge about reality,
especially when the metaphysician starts talking about a
transcendent Absolute. At the same time they feel the need for
an explanation of the fact that in spite of all criticism metaphysics tends to reappear. There are recurrent patterns of
metaphysical thinking which seems to defy the critic's attack.
The people of who I am speaking may indeed think that

linguistic bewitchment plays a part in the production of metaphysical systems, but they also feel that an explanation of metaphysics in terms of this factor alone is too thin to be acceptable. If it were simply a case of logical confusion, it should be easily cured, at least in the case of men whose high level of intelligence is not in question. But if the disease is persistent and does not yield to treatment, what is the explanation? It is reasonable to suppose that behind all linguistic or logical confusion there is some deepseated urge or drive, some factor or factors, deep within the recesses of the human personality, which are responsible for the fact that on some minds at least metaphysics exercises a powerful attraction, whatever broadsides may be fired from time to time by anti-metaphysical critics.

Given the premises, this is a perfectly understandable attitude. But is there a necessary connection between disbelief in the cognitive value of metaphysics and belief in the operation of a drive or unconscious desire of some sort in metaphysical thinking? If so, then to admit that metaphysics is the manifestation of a drive would entail admitting that it has no cognitive value. But I do not think that this is the case.

Let us suppose for the sake of argument that we wish to say with Nietzsche that the pursuit of knowledge, in the sciences for example, is a manifestation of the fundamental will to power. Nietzsche may have gone on in his customarily provocative manner to assert that truth is a biologically useful form of error. But whatever he may have said, our thesis does not necessarily commit us to blurring the distinction between truth and falsehood and asserting that what is called truth is simply a form of error which happens to serve the will to power. For we might very well maintain that it is precisely the striving after the attainment of objective scientific truth which best serves the will to power in this context.

Perhaps I may be pardoned for making my point in a rather more elaborate manner. It is doubtless possible to represent metaphysics as an attempt to satisfy a purely disinterested curiosity, as an attempt, that is, to understand the world simply for the sake of understanding it. Thus according to Whitehead the speculative reason 'seeks with disinterested curiosity an understanding of the world'.[7] True, he maintained that metaphysics rests on an initial act of faith in the intelligibility of the world of empirical fact. But presumably the measure of success achieved by speculative philosophy in its 'endeavour to form a coherent, logical, necessary system of general ideas in terms of which every element of our experience can be interpreted'[8] serves to justify the initial act of faith or hypothesis. In any case the spirit in which the philosopher seeks to understand the world is described by Whitehead as one of disinterested curiosity.

There are, however, those who interpret metaphysics as an instrument in the service of some end—'life' or 'existence', for instance—other than the satisfaction of mere mental curiosity. As an example we can take the late Ortega y Gasset. We may not indeed think of Ortega as being primarily, if at all, a metaphysician. But he had a theory of the vital function of reason which entails a certain view of metaphysical reflection. In his opinion man seeks to understand his historical situation (himself and his 'circumstances') with a view to life. That is to say, man seeks philosophical clarity for the sake of living and acting in the world. Genuine philosophising, as distinct, say, from the mere perpetuation of a certain system or tradition, is always the product of doubt. When the system of beliefs which has formed the more or less unquestioned background of a culture has once been exposed to the corroding effect of criticism and scepticism, so that the unquestioned beliefs become disputable ideas, it becomes necessary to substitute for it a system of rationally grounded ideas. And those who seriously endeavour to fulfil this need are the genuine and original philosophers. Thus when Socrates and Plato endeavoured by means of a system of ideas based on reason to overcome the corroding criticism to which the traditions of ancient Greece had been exposed, they afforded examples of genuine philosophising. They were seeking clarity and knowledge not merely out of curiosity or for the sake of knowledge but rather for the sake of life. Philosophy is justified because it is needed for life.

Are these two interpretations of philosophy so opposed that the one inevitably excludes the other? They can, of course, be so presented that they embody different ideals of human life. This would be the case if we understood the first interpretation as meaning that the withdrawn and solitary contemplation of metaphysical truth is the highest goal of human existence and the second as meaning that self-commitment through action in a social setting is the ideal for man. And the two interpretations are obviously opposed and mutually exclusive if we understand the first as involving the idea of objective truth as the attainable goal of the human mind's search and the second as substituting for this idea a purely pragmatist or instrumentalist concept of truth. But the man who wishes to subordinate philosophy to life can equally well maintain that the clarity which is sought for the sake of life is the clarity of objective truth. The alleged relativism of Ortega is irrelevant here. The point is that the idea of the vital function of reason does not necessarily entail the view that objective truth is unattainable in principle, even if it is not attainable in its entirety and in unalloyed purity by any given finite mind. If we say of an engineer that he seeks knowledge and then add that he seeks it for the sake of its practical utility the second statement does not imply that the knowledge sought for is not real objective knowledge. Similarly, if we first say that the metaphysician seeks to understand the world, and if we then add that he seeks this understanding for the sake of life, the second statement does not necessarily contradict or cancel out the first. Why should it?

The point which I am trying to make is this. Even if it is admitted that behind metaphysics there is a drive of some sort, this admission is not necessarily equivalent to an acknowledgement that metaphysics has no cognitive validity. It may be said that to seek philosophical clarity about the self and its environment for the sake of life may very well be a conscious process. That is to say, the desire of clarity for the sake of life may be a conscious rather than an unconscious desire. Indeed some philosophers have explicitly stressed the practical value of philosophy. This is quite true. But it is possible to maintain, whether rightly or wrongly, that behind the construction of metaphysical systems there lies a vital impulse or urge which impels the philosopher to construct a general world view as a supporting background for a way of life. Obviously, metaphysical reflection is itself a form of life. It cannot be a mere external instrument of a vital impulse: it must be itself a manifestation of the fundamental vital urge. But there is no need to enter upon an exegesis of the vitalistic conception of philosophy. My point is that this interpretation of philosophy does not entail the conclusion that there is no objective truth or that, if there is, philosophy is not concerned with it. It is quite possible to say that the philosopher seeks to understand the world and then to add 'for the sake of life' without being forced by this addition to negate the original statement or to embrace a purely relativistic theory of truth.

Similarly, if I say that metaphysics is a manifestation of the finite spirit's orientation to the Absolute I do not mean that the metaphysician will arrive at certain conclusions under the influence of a blind drive. Let me take an example. I alluded earlier (pp. 105-6) to Wittgenstein's contention that the philosopher's passion for generalisation was a mistake. And against this contention I maintained that 'the tendency towards unification is a manifestation of the general movement of the theoretical reason'. In the context, to understand is to unify, though without the blurring or obliteration of differences. The tendency to unification is inherent in the understanding itself. And I interpret this movement towards unification as a movement towards the Absolute, as a manifestation of the finite spirit's orientation to the Absolute. But it does not follow that any given metaphysician must arrive at certain conclusions. If a man embarks on metaphysics at all, he will indeed strive towards unification of the many. And if he perseveres in metaphysical reflection, he will arrive at some sort of unification. But the type of unification at which he arrives is not the predictable result of a blind drive or urge common to metaphysically minded persons. In other words, if one interprets the movement towards unification as a manifestation of the spirit's orientation to the Absolute, one is putting this movement in a wider setting, but one is not saying that the conscious processes of the metaphysician's mind are no more than the expression of a blind urge, or that what the metaphysician imagined to be a genuine pursuit of objective truth was really only the rationalised expression of a blind drive which obscures intellectual clarity and prevents the proper functioning of the reason.

It may be said, and with justice, that those who speak of powerful drives lying behind metaphysics do not generally mean that a metaphysician's conclusions and his choice of arguments are predetermined by a blind subconscious urge. They mean, for instance, that the fact that monism tends to recur is due to the powerful attraction which it exercises on certain minds, and that this attraction is probably explicable in psychological terms. But it does not follow that the precise kind of monism chosen or the precise arguments adopted by the monist in defence of his position are predictable in terms of some psychological drive alone. It is the attraction towards monism in general which is psychologically explicable. And though the arguments adopted by the monist in defence of his position play a subordinate role in comparison with the attraction which has its roots in the recesses of the personality, it does not follow that their precise nature is predictable in terms of a subconscious desire or urge or drive taken by itself. Hence my remarks about my interpretation of metaphysics as a manifestation of the spirit's orientation to the Absolute not involving the predictability of the conclusions arrived at or of the arguments adopted by the metaphysician are really irrelevant. These facts remain. First, I admit that metaphysics is the expression of something which lies behind metaphysics, deep in the recesses of the human personality. Secondly, instead of leaving the determination of this 'something' to the psychologists I offer a questionable metaphysical theory to account for metaphysics. Thirdly, I ought to admit that in metaphysics argumentation plays a subordinate role in comparison with the drive which I find, rightly or wrongly, behind metaphysics.

Well, I do, of course, admit that metaphysics is in a sense the expression of something which lies behind metaphysics, 'deep in the recesses of the human personality'. For metaphysics is an expression of the finality of finite spirit as such, a finality of which a given metaphysician may or may not be aware. And to this extent I am perfectly willing to admit that argumentation plays a subordinate role. That is to say, arguments in metaphysics can be seen as steps in the actualisation of the spirit's fundamental orientation. At the same time it is important to point out that this admission is not equivalent to saying that the metaphysician cannot help using certain arguments or arriving at certain conclusions. The fact that it is spirit-in-the-world with which we are concerned does indeed predetermine a certain very general pattern of reflection. Reason cannot avoid starting with the empirically given, in fact if not in theory. To arrive at the Absolute it must perform the movement of transcendence. But, of course, it may not arrive there. And even if it performs the movement of transcendence, it may express this movement in the form of either good or bad arguments Under all the arguments, bad as well as good, we can see the finality of spirit; but this does not mean that the arguments are automatically produced expressions of a drive.

The use of the word 'drive' may give an unfortunate impression. The word does indeed seem to be used in a rather loose way, and it may be legitimate to apply it to the orientation of finite spirit to the Absolute. But this is questionable. And in any case its use may tend to give the impression that I am offering my interpretation of metaphysics as a theory which excludes all psychological hypotheses about the influence of subconscious factors on human thought. But this is not the case. My interpretation is concerned with the nature of finite spirit as such rather than with variable psychological factors. Take monism for example. It may be possible to make various sets of statements about it. Some will be statements of philosophical criticism, while others might be psychological statements about the factors which played a part in predisposing the philosopher in question to monism. And both these sets of statements might in principle be true. They are not of necessity mutually exclusive. Nor do they together exclude the statement that monism manifests even if imperfectly, the finality of the finite spirit as such. Nor does this last statement exclude the two sets mentioned. In principle at least all are compatible. In other words, while my interpretation of metaphysics in terms of the spirit's finality rules out the adequacy of an explanation of metaphysics in purely psychoanalytic terms, it does not exclude the possibility of psychologists making true and pertinent statements about this or that metaphysician. After all, meta-physicians are not pure spirits; they are human beings.

As for my interpretation of metaphysics being a questionable theory, I certainly do not expect it to be accepted without more ado. It is in the actual process of metaphysical reflection that spirit comes to recognise its own finality, as far as philosophy is concerned. Finite spirit goes out of itself in its search for reality or being. It performs, or can perform, the movement of transcendence and conceive the transcendent Absolute. It can then recognise the whole process of reflection as one of the ways in which its own finality is manifested. It becomes conscious of itself as finite spirit orientated to the infinite Spirit in which it is grounded. I am thus prepared to admit that metaphysics is in some sense the self-reflection of spirit, provided that this idea of metaphysics is not taken to mean that that which spirit recognises is a purely subjective tendency or drive rather than its orientation to an objective reality. Even so, some of those who sympathise with my general account of metaphysics may object that the emphasis is misplaced. They may suggest, that is to say, that the emphasis should be placed on the transcendent object of knowledge rather than on spirit's recognition of its own finality. But, be this as it may, the point which I am trying to bring out is that it is only in and through the actual process of metaphysical reflection, culminating in the attempt to grasp the Absolute through the web of our analogical concepts, that the wider significance of the process is recognised by the finite spirit, in terms of its own inner finality.[9] To the outsider, so to speak, my interpretation of metaphysics as a manifestation of the finite spirit's orientation to the Absolute may very well appear at best as a gratuitous assumption and at worst as nonsense. It is in and through its own performance of the movement of transcendence that the spirit comes to recognise the meaning of its own striving. This knowledge is prefigured, as it were, in the structure of the spirit, but it is not there explicitly from the start. It is rendered explicit and appropriated only in the process of personal reflection which constitutes the recognition of an already existing ontological relationship. If anyone wishes to call this idea of metaphysics 'mystical', it does not matter to me, provided that it is understood that I am speaking of the movement of reflection and not of supernaturally infused mystical knowledge.

v

It will be remembered that my imagined critic referred to the concept of satisfaction. He remarked that with Spinoza I feel that only 'a thing eternal and infinite' can satisfy my desire. And he went on to say, 'You are therefore impelled by dissatisfaction with the finite to proceed further, to perform what you call the movement of transcendence.' He went on to maintain that this dissatisfaction with the finite makes sense only if it is assumed that there must be an infinite Absolute. 'And this assumption is the expression of the heart's desire.'

From what I have said in this chapter it should be clear that I am prepared to admit that there is a measure of truth in the critic's contentions. If the finite spirit is indeed orientated to the infinite Absolute, it follows that only the infinite can satisfy it. And if metaphysics is one way that this orientation is manifested, it follows that the movement of transcendence can be regarded as proceeding from spirit's dissatisfaction with the finite. But it does not follow that it is all a question of the heart's desire, if this is taken to mean an emotional longing for the infinite. There is, I think, a tendency towards the infinite which precedes metaphysical reflection and is manifested in it. And inasmuch as the philosopher is a man, a human being, and not pure reason, we can hardly deny the possibility of his being influenced by other factors than purely rational considerations. At the same time metaphysical reflection as such is reflection, a movement of reason, and the dissatisfaction with the finite is primarily, as far as metaphysics is concerned, an intellectual dissatisfaction. The movement of transcendence satisfies the reason in the sense that it responds to the demands of reason, not merely in the sense that it satisfies 'the heart's desire'.

The critic also referred to Bradley's assertion that 'the want of an object, and, still, more, the search for an object, imply in a certain sense the knowledge of that object'. And while recognising that my idea of the Absolute differs from that of Bradley, he suggested that this quotation represents my attitude. Well, I cannot embark here on a discussion of the meaning which Bradley intended this passage to bear. But I think that I have made it clear that if I regard metaphysics as in some sense a search for the Absolute, I do not consider that the search necessarily presupposes any determinate idea of the Absolute. A man may say, 'I don't really know what I want,' or 'I don't really know what I am looking for.' Of course, in a sense he does know, but in an indeterminate way. He may be looking for satisfaction or for happiness: but he does not know precisely what will satisfy him or what will confer happiness. The metaphysician may be in an analogous situation. He looks for reality, for being, but he does not know where to locate it, so to speak. 'What nonsense!' someone may say. 'It is there in the things to hand.' Well, the metaphysician does indeed turn first to the things at hand, just as the man who is seeking happiness turns first to the things at hand. But he may find himself impelled to perform the movement of transcendence. That he is searching at all is due to his nature as spirit. That he turns to the things at hand is due to the fact that he is spirit-in-the-world.

This somewhat protracted discussion of the role of desire in metaphysics may have made the reader impatient. He may wonder when, if ever, I propose to give a more systematic account of the movement of transcendence to which I have so frequently referred. But I shall begin treating this theme in the next chapter. In view of the fact that according to me the human spirit is orientated to the Absolute, it might perhaps be expected that I should attempt to argue directly from the need of or from an unconscious desire of the Absolute to the existence of the Absolute. But this is not the line of argument which I propose to emphasise. I do not, indeed, regard the argument from need and unconscious desire as deserving the contempt which it sometimes meets. It is easy to say, for instance, that the desire for air does not prove that there is air. But it is also easy to retort that though my present desire for air does not prove that air is here and now available (for I might be suffocating from want of it), the fact that the human organism needs air to live at all does show that there is such a thing. And one might develop this line of thought. It does not seem to me that the retort just mentioned suffices to show that the line of thought is sound when applied to the problem of the Absolute. For there are notable differences between the two cases, and these differences must be taken into account. But it may be possible to make something of the argument from need or unconscious desire. However, be this as it may, I have explained that in my opinion it is in and through its own performance of the movement of transcendence that the spirit comes to recognise the meaning of its own striving. And I have also indicated that by the movement of transcendence I mean the movement by which reflective reason transcends the world towards an Absolute which is not identifiable with the world. Hence I shall be concerned in the next chapter with the idea of the world and with the movement by which the mind transcends the world.

9
The movement of transcendence

L E T us assume from the start the level of consciousness at which the human being finds himself in a world which comprises many things besides himself. As I-subject the human being can be said to *find* himself in a world. As object to himself he can be said to find *himself* in a world. This world comprises a multiplicity of persons and things. The idea of the world which I assume is a primitive idea, formed in close dependence on sense-experience. We are aware of things as distinct from one another, but not as entirely unrelated. We are aware of them, for instance, as spatially and temporally related. This tree is near that one in comparison with its distance from some other tree. This event precedes or follows that one. The level of consciousness which I assume is not a level at which there are only unrelated distinct things: there is a general unifying situation, the world, the idea of which is grounded in my personal sense-experience.

The word 'assume' may give rise to misunderstanding. It is not meant to indicate any doubt on my part about the existence of persons and things distinct from myself. I have no intention of starting from the Cartesian Cogito and then trying to prove the existence of an extra-mental world. The word 'assume' is meant to indicate that I presuppose a certain level of consciousness, leaving questions about its genesis to the psychologists.

These remarks should not be taken to mean that I assume that the mind is first confronted with purely discrete impressions, and that I leave it to the psychologists to investigate the work of synthesis which precedes the emergence of the level of consciousness which I presuppose or start from. The emphasis

which I have laid and shall continue to lay on the unifying
activity of the mind may give the impression that this is what
I do mean. But in point of fact I do not. It might be claimed
that we are not first confronted with a multiplicity of purely
discrete phenomena, but that we come to distinguish things
through their different relations to ourselves and to one
another. Awareness of distinctness and awareness of relatedness
arise together, it might be said. I have no wish to deny this.
I simply leave these psychological questions to the psychologists
and assume, presuppose or start from, the level of consciousness
at which the human being can be said to find himself in a
world which comprises many other things besides himself.

II

At the same time, even if the level of consciousness which
I assume or presuppose is not a level at which there are
entirely unrelated distinct things, the mind, in its process of
understanding the world, carries unification further than the
unification which is already present at this presupposed level
of consciousness. This is obviously the case in science where
the process of generalisation unifies phenomena within the
field of the science in question.

   Now, I have said on a former occasion that reason seeks
to unify the many given in experience—that is, at the level of
consciousness which I presuppose. What do I mean by reason
in this context? I mean the human mind as directed towards the
theoretical understanding of the world of persons and things,
even if this understanding is subordinated to an ulterior aim
which is not simply that of satisfying mental curiosity. Quite
apart from the question of spirit's final end, I might have a
'practical' aim in view. But the attainment of this practical
aim may demand previous theoretical understanding. And I
call the mind 'reason' as directed towards this understanding.
If, therefore, I speak of reason as doing this or that, I am
speaking of the human mind as engaged in a certain activity
in a certain context, irrespective of the number of people who
engage in this activity or of the assiduity with which any given
individual engages in it. When terms such as 'reason' or 'mind'
function as subjects in sentences, they do not signify all men at

all times. References to cavemen or to rock 'n' roll performers are thus irrelevant. To speak in a manner reminiscent of Locke in his polemic against the theory of innate ideas, I am aware of the interests of babies, of savage hunters in the primeval forests, of football players and lovers, of metaphysicians when they are playing bridge or visiting the cinema. I am not ignorant of the fact that the mind functions in ways other than that which I call reason or theoretical reason.

Why does the theoretical reason seek to unify the manifold, the many? As asked by me, this question can be made to appear absurd. I have just described reason, as I use the term in the present context, as the mind directed towards the understanding of the world. And I asserted earlier (p. 138) that in the context understanding involves unification. Hence if I now ask why reason seeks to unify the manifold, it might be argued that the question is, for me, at least, equivalent to asking why understanding seeks to understand. And there does not seem to be much point in such a question. At the same time we can legitimately ask for a justification of the statement that in the context to understand is or involves unification.

In answer, one might point out that in common usage to understand an event means, or at least often means, knowing or discovering its cause or causes. Thus we can be said to understand the movement of the blind when we notice that the window is open and that a breeze is blowing in. Here we have a case of linking one phenomenon with another in a causal relationship and to this extent of unification or bringing together. Again, there are circumstances in which we can be said to understand an action when we know the motive of the agent and when we can see the action as fitting in with the pattern of the agent's known character. 'I can't understand his action. It seems so unlike him to act in this way.' 'Oh, but his motive was not what you probably think it was. He acted in this way because he thought it would help X.' 'Well, in that case I understand his action.' I say that I understand the action when I see it in the light of the agent's motive and known character, when it is seen in a certain setting, when a work of linking-up or unification has been performed. On a broader scale it could be pointed out that to understand a historical movement involves unifying in various ways a great number of historical facts: it involves unification in the sense of seeing connections, relations, a pattern.

I certainly should not be so bold as to assert dogmatically that there are no exceptions to this sort of use of 'understanding' in common usage. But some cases at any rate which may appear at first sight to constitute exceptions may turn out on closer examination not to do so. 'I don't understand this word.' What do I fail to understand? Its meaning, of course. Yes, but its meaning is explained by its being shown how the word functions in the language to which it belongs. Coming to understand the word involves seeing it in a certain setting or framework: it involves what can be called unification. Again, 'I don't understand this letter.' This sentence might have various meanings. But let us assume that it means that I fail to understand why the writer wrote as he did, what he was getting at, what his intentions were. In this case I understand the letter when I understand why it was written. That is to say, I understand it when it has been placed in a context, when a work of unification has been performed. But examples might be multiplied indefinitely.

I have appealed to common usage in support of the contention that in the context of the activity of theoretical reason, understanding involves unification. But it might be objected that the appeal to common usage is inadequate. Obviously, the suggestion is not that common usage is wrong, in the sense that it does not reveal the customary range of meaning of 'understanding'. For if this customary range of meaning is not embodied in our ordinary language, where on earth is it to be found? Nor is the objection which I have in mind equivalent to the suggestion that we ought to revise common usage, that is, that we ought to mean by understanding something other than what we customarily mean by it or that we ought, for some reason or other, to restrict the application of the term to one particular part of the total range of meaning which it ordinarily bears and which is expressed in common usage. There is therefore no need to discuss here the case for and against the revision of language by philosophers. I do not mean by this remark that I condemn or reject such revision in principle. I mean that there is no need to discuss the matter here because the objection which I have in mind does not amount to a contention that common usage ought to be revised or that philosophers ought to develop a special usage of their own. The objection which I have in mind is that the appeal to common usage is inadequate in the sense that we can still go on to ask what insight finds expression in common usage. Some might wish to claim that if it makes sense to speak of an insight being expressed in common usage, it can be revealed only by describing common usage. But the counter-claim might be made that it is possible for an insight to find expression in common usage in the sense that it is implied by concrete ways of speech, though it does not find expression in the sense of explicit statement. In this case what is required is not simply a describing of common usage but a reflecting on it. The appeal to common usage would then be inadequate if it stopped at surface-description, so to speak, though it would still be useful.

For my own part I agree with this objection. That is to say I think that the uses of 'understanding' which I have illustrated from our ordinary language imply an insight which underlies, as it were, these uses and which reflection can bring to light. But I prefer to postpone explanations of what I consider this insight to be, as this will enable me to avoid a certain amount of repetition at a later stage of the discussion. I mention the point here simply in order to make it plain that my appeal to common usage does not mean that I regard such appeals as the final stage in philosophical reflection. At the same time I hope that the appeal has been of use in showing that the view that reason's activity of understanding the world involves unification is not a strange and monstrous paradox, contrary to all that we ordinarily understand by 'understanding'.

III

At this point there are two further remarks which I wish to make about reason's activity of unification.

First, in the examples which I have given unification involves relating, but not the obliteration of the unified. That is, what is said to be understood is not merged without trace in some whole. The movement of the blind retains, as it were, its identity when it is seen as an effect of the blowing of the breeze.

The action which is said to be understood is not annulled by being seen in the light of the agent's motive and known character. Individual historical facts do not simply disappear when they are linked together to form the pattern of a general movement. A strange word still remains a distinct symbol when it is understood in terms of its function or functions in a certain language. In other words, by unification of the manifold I do not mean the dissolution of all distinction, individuality and differentiating factors.

Secondly, in the example of the relating of the blind's movement to the blowing of the breeze one phenomenon is linked with another. And this causal explanation satisfies anyone who is merely wondering why the blind is making an irritating noise by its movement. For it is sufficient to enable him to take the necessary steps to remove the cause of his irritation. But though the explanation is quite sufficient for this practical purpose, the linking of phenomenon A with phenomenon B does not satisfy theoretical reason as such. On this plane reason cannot stop at any given point. The picture of the world as a linear succession of phenomena is scarcely adequate. But let us overlook this inadequacy. We can then say that if reason relates A to B, it is then impelled to relate B to C, and so on indefinitely. Underlying this movement of reason I see the orientation of spirit to the infinite. But we have not yet introduced the notion of transcendence. And on the level at which we find ourselves the movement takes the form of indefinite progression.

Let us put these two ideas together. Reason strives to understand the world, and this understanding involves unification. But, as we have seen, unification is not the same thing as conflation. Reason demands unification without suppression of the many. The temptation may, of course, arise to sacrifice either differentiation to unification or unification to differentiation. On the one hand the mind may be so impressed by unifying factors that it comes to embrace an extreme monism. On the other hand it may be so impressed by individuality and differentiating factors that it is led to embrace an extreme form of nominalism. The ideal, however, is that of unification without the sacrifice of individuality and differentiation. But this unification remains an ideal. On the level which we are considering reason moves indefinitely along the path to complete unification, and so to complete understanding.

IV

This idea of the system of interrelated material things is what I mean by the idea of the world in the present context. The term 'world' can obviously bear various meanings. In certain contexts it may mean our planet, as it generally does if we speak of a journey round the world. In other contexts it may have a moral and spiritual meaning, as when someone speaks of the world, the flesh and the devil. Both these meanings are excluded in the present context.

The content of one's idea of the world is, in an obvious sense, variable. The content of an educated man's idea of the world differs in obvious ways from the content of the idea which he had when a small child. But there is no need to dwell on this point. I ought, however, to explain briefly what I mean by saying that I am using the term in the sense of the system of interrelated material things. That is to say, I ought to explain that I am not excluding man from the world. I have indeed maintained that as spirit man stands back from or out of the world, that he is an 'ecstatic being' (see p. 117). But I have also insisted that man is spirit-in-the-world. If he were pure spirit he would not be in the world according to my use of the term 'world' in the present context. But he is not pure spirit. And in virtue of his embodied character he is in the world. If therefore we bear in mind the fact that the description is not intended to exclude man from all participation in the world, we can describe the world as the system of interrelated material things. It is unnecessary to say 'finite' as well as 'material'; for what else can a material thing be but finite?

Now, reason moves towards complete understanding of the world, and so towards complete unification. But, as manifested in science, the activity of reason cannot achieve this complete unification. For though we use the general term 'science', science takes the form of the particular sciences. And the unification achieved by any one particular science is necessarily only partial. Hence the unifying activity of reason, though manifested in science, is not exhausted by it. And in metaphysical philosophy it strives after a completer unification, a completer understanding.

This activity of reason is in my opinion quite right and proper. It may be said that reason should content itself with trying to unify the conclusions and hypotheses of the sciences. And no doubt it can try to do this. But there may very well be aspects of the world, of things, which reflective reason regards as important but which lie outside the scope of the particular sciences. In this way 'descriptive metaphysics' arises.

But while it is quite proper for reason to pursue its unifying activity outside or beyond the limits of the particular sciences, it runs a risk when it does so. And the risk which I have in mind is that of succumbing to the temptation of absolutising the world, of conceiving it, that is to say, as a self-sufficient absolute entity or super-substance.

The force of the temptation is easily understandable if one accepts my interpretation of metaphysics as one of the ways in which the orientation of the finite spirit to the infinite Absolute is manifested. At least it is easily understandable if one bears in mind my earlier contention that metaphysics does not necessarily presuppose a determinate idea of the Absolute (p. 132). For the mind, encountering the manifold given in experience and setting out on a path of indefinite unification, is naturally tempted to locate its goal in the system in which the subject finds itself, the horizons of which always recede. A metaphysician who sets out to locate, as it were, ultimate reality, without any previous determinate idea of it, is naturally tempted to absolutise in some way the world-system, conceiving it as the ultimate self-sufficient reality, the Absolute. In virtue of his fundamental orientation to the Absolute his reason, in its process of unification, moves towards the Absolute. And the temptation arises, to express the matter rather crudely, to accept the first plausible candidate which comes to hand.

But to understand the temptation it is not necessary to accept in advance my interpretation of metaphysics as a manifestation of the orientation of the finite spirit to the Absolute. Let us assume that the world is a system of things. And let us consider one particular thing, a man for example. For continued life he is dependent on air, among other things. And the presence of air is dependent on other factors, and so on. Now, it is clear that the system which comprises all these things cannot itself be dependent in the same sense in which one member of the system is dependent on other members. And it is tempting to draw the conclusion that the system must be independent in the sense that it is absolutely self-sufficient. The conclusion does not in fact follow, but it may seem to follow.

It may occur to the reader that I ought to refer to the influence of linguistic bewitchment in connection with our use of the term 'world'. But it seems correct to say that those who maintain that philosophers are sometimes bewitched by our use of this term are generally concerned to argue that our use of the noun 'world' facilitates or insinuates the idea of the world as a limited whole, an idea which may then be employed as basis for an argument for the existence of God. And this is not what I mean by the absolutisation of the world. To absolutise the world is to blow it up, so to speak, into a self-sufficient reality, not to reduce it to a limited, finite entity. To absolutise the world is not, for instance, to assign it a temporal beginning, quite the contrary.

It may be said, of course, that the real point which those who speak of the bewitching influence of the term 'world' wish to make is that our use of the noun facilitates or insinuates the idea of the world as a thing, whereas in fact it is not a thing at all, either infinite or finite, necessary or contingent, self-sufficient or dependent. But this is a line of thought to which I shall return presently. At the moment I only wish to remark that while I have no intention of denying that the structure and forms of language can influence thought, I think that this influence can be, and sometimes is, exaggerated. And I do not believe that what I have called the absolutisation of the world is a simple case of linguistic bewitchment. I think that it is something much more complicated.

v

In the last section I spoke of the risk of succumbing to a temptation, namely that of absolutising the world. But it is not inevitable that the metaphysician should succumb to this temptation. If I depict reason as first absolutising the world and then performing a work of reductive analysis, I am not suggesting that reason always proceeds in this way when it

embarks on metaphysics. For the matter of that I do not intend
to suggest that every metaphysician feels a strong temptation
to conceive the world as the self-sufficient absolute reality.
He may, for example, start with such a firm belief, derived from
extra-philosophical sources, in a transcendent Absolute, that
he has little or no inclination to conceive the world in this way.
Or he may be so impressed by distinction and differences that
his reflections take the form of a 'dissolution' of the world
rather than of an absolutisation of it. And even when the
temptation to absolutise the world does arise, it may be
occasioned by reflections other than those which I have already
mentioned. For instance, if a philosopher starts with the
conviction that there is an infinite reality, and if he lacks any
clear idea of the analogy of being, he may draw the conclusion
that there can be only one Being, the Absolute in the form of
the universe.

In other words, I am concerned here with outlining a certain
dialectic of the reason, proceeding through successive moments.
And I hope in this way to exhibit the world in a certain light
and to show that the movement of transcendence is less like
an irrational leap than it is sometimes supposed to be. But I am
not concerned with history, in the sense of outlining a path
of reflection which has been followed, in all its successive stages,
by every metaphysician of the past. My dialectic has, of course,
a connection with history in the sense that it is possible to find
in the history of philosophy systems which correspond more or
less to this or that moment of the dialectic. But history as such
is not my concern here. For the matter of that, it is not my
intention to suggest that every metaphysician ought to follow
the path of my dialectic. I do not wish to say, for example, that
every metaphysician ought first to absolutise the world and then,
if I may be permitted such verbal barbarity, to de-absolutise
it. I am outlining a certain possible dialectic of reason with a
view to illuminating the movement of transcendence as I
conceive it. But there are doubtless other ladders which can
be used to make the ascent.

VI

Resuming the theme of the world, we might begin by considering the statement that the world is not a thing but the

class of things. If this statement were taken to mean that the term 'world' is a name given to an indefinite number of purely discrete entities, so that the world would be reducible to unrelated things, it would scarcely be an adequate account of the world. The world can no more be reduced to an indefinite number of finite things considered as unrelated entities than the word 'Russia', in the sentence 'Russia attacked Finland', can be reduced to individual Russians considered purely as discrete entities. Clearly, the military operation against Finland was planned and carried out by individuals. But it was not planned and carried out by them simply as unrelated individuals. If we wished to translate the sentence 'Russia attacked Finland' into a set of sentences in which the word Russia would not appear but only individual Russians would be mentioned, the translation would hardly be adequate unless the relations between the Russians who were in any way involved were also mentioned. Analogously, the world is not reducible without residue to unrelated finite things. The idea of system, of interrelation, seems to be essential to our idea of the world.

Let us assume therefore that the world can be described as the spatio-temporal system. This system is not nothing; it is a real system. And it is obviously a totality, a whole. To say this does not commit us to saying that the world is a limited whole, in the sense, for example, that there is a first ideally assignable moment of the world's history. This question is left entirely open. If we wish to look on the world as a series of interrelated phenomena, we can say that it is the whole series without committing ourselves to completing the series in the sense of asserting that it had a first member.

Now, if the world is a real developing system, an evolving totality in some sense, we may be inclined to say that it is a thing or an entity, on the ground that it is not nothing. And perhaps there is no harm in speaking in this way provided that we remember that we are using the term 'thing' in an analogous sense. For the spatio-temporal system of interrelated material things cannot be a thing in precisely the same sense in which its members are things. We could not properly enumerate the things which in various relations form the world and then mention the world itself as an additional member of the series. This is the point, or one of them, which is brought out by the statement that the world is not a thing but the class of things.

If we bear this in mind, we can speak of the world as a thing or entity without drawing the conclusion that the attributes of the things which in their relations compose the world can legitimately be predicated of the world itself. At the same time our way of speaking may easily incline us to assume that the opposites of the attributes which the members of the system have in common can legitimately be predicated of the world. The point can be brought out by employing Scholastic language. Let us suppose that we describe the members of the world-system as 'contingent beings'. And let us also suppose not only that we agree about not predicating of the system itself the common attributes of its members but also that we wish to call the world a being. We shall not then call it a contingent being. But if we call it a being at all, we may easily draw the conclusion that the world must have the opposite attribute and that it is a necessary being.

Of course, if we accept the statement that the world is not a thing but the class of things, we shall not be inclined to draw this conclusion. The class of sheep is not a sheep. But it is not any other kind of animal either; it is not an animal at all. Similarly, if the world is the class of contingent beings, it is not itself a contingent being. But neither is it a necessary being. It is not 'a being' at all, whether contingent or necessary. At the same time the world is not nothing; it is a real system. And we have admitted that it might be said to be a thing or entity, provided that we remembered that the term was being used in an analogous sense.

We may appear to have landed ourselves in a contradictory position. But let us ask what the term 'thing' means if it is applied to the world in an analogous sense. What is its cash-value? It means, as had been already remarked, that the world is not nothing, but a real system. A system of what? Of things. And to say that it is a system of things is to say that it is reducible to things and relations. It is not something over and above interrelated things. The absolutisation of the world depends on our conceiving the world, at least implicitly, as being something over and above the interrelated things which compose it. And if this way of conceiving the world is rejected, the absolutisation of the world is also rejected.

If anyone is prepared to maintain that the world is a super-organism with a soul of its own, a world-soul, he will indeed also be prepared to maintain that it is something over and above the things which in their various relations are said to be in the world. But though the hypothesis of a world-soul has a long history and is not without interest, it is not a hypothesis which I feel disposed to accept. So I propose to take it that the world is reducible to things and relations, and that if it is called a thing, we mean, or ought to mean, by this no more than that the world is a real system of things. This is not indeed altogether satisfactory I must admit. In particular, the concept of 'thing' is left undefined and vague. But if I am to succeed in giving a general picture of my line of thought, I must pass over this theme. The main point I wish to make is that the world is not something over and above its contents—over and above, that is, what is said to be 'in the world'. This phrase tends to suggest that the world is an entity which transcends the things said to be in it. But the phrase can be interpreted in terms of the relations between things.

VII

Let us carry the matter further. I have said that the world is reducible to things and relations. The things are all existentially unstable. True, some things last much longer than others. We may speak sometimes of 'the eternal hills'. But we do not take the phrase literally. Everywhere in the spatio-temporal system there is change, instability, insecurity. To kill a human being is easy enough from a temporal point of view; to split the atom is a difficult operation. But in principle every material thing is existentially unstable. As for the relations between things, they are contingent. And it is on this point that I wish to reflect.

There is obviously a sense in which it is true to say that a human being cannot exist without oxygen. If he is deprived of all oxygen a man dies. But there is no logical contradiction between a statement affirming the existence of a human being and a statement denying the presence of oxygen (unless, of course, we choose to induce a logical contradiction by including the presence of oxygen in a man's lungs as part of the meaning of the statement that a human being exists). In general, when X is one finite thing and Y is another finite thing, there is no logical contradiction involved in affirming X and denying Y or in affirming Y and denying X. And in this case it is logically possible for there to be an X without a Y. And if there is as a matter of fact a relation of dependence between them, this relation is contingent.

Now, I have spoken of 'logical contradiction' and 'logical possibility'. But I prefer to say that when X is one finite thing and Y is another finite thing, there is no metaphysical impossibility in there being an X when there is no Y, even though as a matter of physical fact X depends on Y. To put the matter in general and plain terms, there is no metaphysical impossibility in X existing without the rest of the spatio-temporal system on which, as a matter of empirical fact, it depends. All the relations between the distinct members of the world are contingent relations.

The world is thus reducible to existentially unstable things and contingent relations. From the physical point of view the world presents itself to us as a massive system of things interrelated in such a way that the presence of the system is a necessary condition for the existence of any member. And in its process of unification without obliteration of distinctions reason may be tempted to absolutise the world as a One-in-Many. That is to say, it may be tempted to give content to Being or Reality in the form of the total system of interrelated things. conceived as a self-sufficient developing unity. But from the metaphysical point of view the world falls apart, as it were, into finite things, each of which is existentially unstable, and contingent relations.

We thus have two moments of dialectic. Reason unifies the manifold in the idea of the world, which it may then absolutise. It then performs a reductive analysis which, while not of course denying the physical system, resolves the unity, from a metaphysical point of view, into multiplicity. But before I can exhibit reason in the movement of transcendence I must discuss briefly a further point.

VIII

In the last section I said that the relations between the members of the world-system are contingent, and that it is metaphysically possible for a given member to exist without the rest of the spatio-temporal system. Now I assert that the completely isolated finite thing is unintelligible. That is to say, reason cannot remain in the idea of such an individual; it has to relate it to something else as ground of its existence. To understand the finite existent involves this relating. This is, I think, the insight which is implied by our ordinary use of 'understanding'. It is an insight into the nature of finite being. It may be said that it is a matter of insight into the truth of certain 'ultimate principles'. But though I have certainly no wish to deny the principles, they themselves must ultimately rest on an insight into the nature of being, unless we are prepared to say that there are subsistent principles hanging about in a world of their own and awaiting discovery. Further, the mind can enjoy the insight without explicitly formulating the principles.

By the completely isolated finite thing I mean a finite thing existing in a void of being or reality, without any relation to any other being whatsoever. In a certain sense the completely isolated individual is conceivable. That is to say we can talk about it; we can approach the idea of it by positively thinking away every other being whatsoever. But it is unthinkable in the sense that reason cannot remain in the idea. The completely isolated finite thing appears to reason as a 'monster', as something which has to be overcome by unification. I do not mean, of course, that we actually encounter the completely isolated finite thing. I mean that when reason approaches the idea and tries to hold it, it cannot remain there but seeks to annul the isolation. If one does not do this, one simply abandons the activity of reason; one renounces understanding. And one is free to do this, of course. But if one does not renounce understanding, reason seeks to annul the isolation. And I do not think that this is simply a matter of psychological custom and association. By speaking of 'insight' I have already indicated this.

IX

What I have just been saying may seem to contradict what was said in the previous section. First I asserted that the relations between members of the spatio-temporal system are contingent, and that it is metaphysically possible for a human being, for instance, to exist without the rest of the world-system.

Then I went on to maintain that the completely isolated finite thing is unintelligible; that it is unthinkable, in the sense that reason cannot remain in the idea but strives, in the process of understanding, to annul the isolation. Hence it may appear to the reader that I have said both that the completely isolated individual is possible and that it is impossible, both that it is thinkable and that it is unthinkable. And what is this but a flagrant self-contradiction?

There is indeed an apparent or *prima facie* contradiction. But a real contradiction arises only if the following condition is fulfilled. The statement that it is metaphysically possible for there to be an X, when X is a finite thing, without the spatio-temporal system must be equivalent to or entail the statement that there can be an X when X is a completely isolated finite thing existing in a total void of being. Let us suppose, however, that X, a finite thing, is so related to a Being which transcends the spatio-temporal system that it is metaphysically possible for this Being to originate and sustain X without the spatio-temporal system, though it is not possible for X to exist unless so originated and sustained. In this case there is no contradiction between the statement that it is metaphysically possible for X to exist without the spatio-temporal system and the statement that it is not possible for X to exist when X is a completely isolated finite thing existing in a total void of being.

The point I am trying to make is, of course, that reason overcomes the apparent or *prima facie* contradiction by performing the movement of transcendence. But to keep the argument within due limits I must break off here. Later, I shall be able to allow my imagined critic or alter ego to have his say. Meanwhile I should like to remind the reader that I am concerned simply with exhibiting a certain dialectical movement. Needless to say, I think that it is a rational process. But I do not present it as a substitute for all other lines of reflection which include the movement of transcendence.

10

Some objections considered

I T may help to clarify the line of thought adumbrated in the last chapter if I reintroduce my imagined critic, my *alter ego*, and give him the opportunity of raising an important objection. In this section, therefore it will be the critic who is speaking.

'The first moment of your dialectic is one of synthesis or unification. According to you the manifold presented in experience is unified by the mind in the ideas of the world. The world is the system of interrelated finite things.[1] You then go on to maintain that the mind tends, or may tend, to absolutise this system, regarding it not only as something which is more than the sum of its members but also as a self-sufficient developing whole or totality, an Absolute.

'In your opinion this tendency is misguided. Hence the second moment of your dialectic is one of analysis. That is to say, you introduce a counter-movement of reason, the movement of reductive analysis, whereby the world is dissolved into an indefinite plurality of finite things and contingent relations. To express the matter linguistically, you maintain that the term 'world' does not signify a super-thing transcending interrelated finite things, but that it is a name for the complex of individual finite things and the relations between them, these relations being contingent.

'If I understand you correctly, you go on to maintain that reason is thus brought into a state of oscillation in which it fails to find what it is seeking. To understand the manifold involves unification. The preliminary unification is achieved in the idea of the world. But this unity dissolves under analysis into the very plurality which reason seeks to unify. Reason is therefore driven to find the unification which it seeks by relating the manifold to a transcendent One, a transcendent Absolute, And the movement of transcendence thus constitutes the third main moment of your dialectic.

'Now, there are several objections which can be brought against this line of argument. Let us suppose that your analysis of the term "the world" is substantially correct. What does it achieve? The answer is simple. It achieves a clarification of the meaning of a term, namely "the world". But while it shows that the world is not a super-thing, distinct from and transcending the finite things which we are accustomed to describe as being in the world, it by no means follows that reason has any adequate ground for performing the movement of transcendence. There is, in my opinion, a concealed ground, namely the assumption that there must be a unity of a kind which is not verified in the world. But this ground, precisely because it is an assumption, is not an adequate ground. It may indeed be adequate from the point of view of mystical faith, but it is not so from the point of view of a philosopher who wishes to rely on logical thinking alone.

'Suppose that I were to criticise your position in this way. It isreasonable to say that in the process of understanding the world, reason is stimulated by a regulative or heuristic idea or an ideal of unity. But this idea receives its content through the unification which is actually achieved by the sciences, a unification which is never complete or final. And the fact that we only approximate to the ideal unification by a process which takes place on the horizontal level, so to speak, constitutes no cogent ground for performing the vertical movement of transcendence.

'You would probably answer that I had misunderstood your position. For you do not argue that we must postulate a transcendent Absolute because scientific unification remains incomplete. The metaphysician, according to you, is concerned with the existence of the finite. The mind's natural tendency is to ground the existence of the finite in the world, by relating individual finite existents to the system. But under analysis the world dissolves into the very things the existence of which has to be grounded. Hence reason must seek a transcendent ground of existence.

'If you replied in this way, your answer would be true, in the sense that it would represent what is actually your line of thought. But do you not see that even in this case you are simply assuming that there must be a ground of existence transcending finite things, a ground of existence to which the indefinite plurality of finite things can be related, as dependent on it? You may say that finite existence must be 'explicable', that it must be rendered 'intelligible'. But in saying this you tacitly assume that there must be an explanation other than the empirical explanation with which you are for some reason or other dissatisfied. Your assumption may perhaps be justified in fact. I am certainly not prepared to state dogmatically that it is not. For I do not know this. But it remains an assumption. It is a matter of initial faith, if you like. This faith may be justified. But it cannot be proved. For it underlies and is presupposed by all so-called proofs.

'At the same time I admit that any plausibility which your line of argument possesses derives very largely from your reductive analysis of the term "world". For you reduce the world to an indefinite plurality of separate finite things, each of which is existentially unstable, and contingent relations. And once the world has been interpreted in this way, the statement that we must look outside it for a ground of existence acquires a certain plausibility. But though for the sake of argument I have been willing to assume up to now that your analysis is substantially correct, it seems to me to be open to criticism. And I wish to outline very briefly a possible line of criticism and to indicate its importance.

'In your approach you seem to presuppose the priority of separate things. You construct from them the idea of the world, and then you resolve the world once more into the things from which it is supposed to be constructed. But one might very well argue that things must be reduced to the world rather than the other way round. That is to say, it might well be argued that what we call "things" are so many forms or configurations assumed by some common element or energy or what not in the evolutionary process. In other words, we might start with unity rather than with plurality and interpret the latter as due to the self-differentiation of the former. True, it would not follow that the world is a super-thing in addition to what we normally look on as things. To this extent at least your reductive analysis would still be valid. But instead of the picture of the world dissolving into isolated finite things and contingent relations we should have the picture of one dynamic process of self-differentiation. And this view of the world seems to me more reasonable than the view of it as a collection of isolated finite things. After all, you yourself see the impossibility of reducing the world simply and solely to atomic individuals. Relations have to be allowed for. But the world does not consist of things which arise out of nothing and disappear into nothing and which, while they exist, are linked by relations. Things are secondary or subordinate to a unified developing process. There is, of course, a sense in which it is true to say that the world is a system of things and not something over and above and distinct from them. But it does not follow that it can be adequately described in terms which imply that it is the result of an addition sum. It is an organic developing process which differentiates itself into things, reassumes them into itself and brings forth new things.

'Please do not misunderstand me, I do not suggest that the adoption of this point of view would necessarily involve the exclusion of all metaphysics. For it would still be open to you to try to display a comprehensive pattern in the evolutionary process. You might wish to argue, for instance, that the process is working towards a goal, that it is a teleological process. But though this goal would transcend any stage yet attained, it would not be a transcendent Absolute in the sense in which you use the term. Suppose, for example, that you wish to argue that the world is moving towards the ideal of complete self-knowledge in and through man. The world would then be itself the Absolute, which moves towards the actualisation of what it always is potentially.

'To sum up, I think that it is in any case very difficult for you to show that what you call the movement of transcendence is required on purely rational grounds. But it becomes even harder if you are willing to admit the inadequacy of your analysis, of the term "world" and to adopt the point of view which I have suggested. For this point of view excludes the reduction of the world to isolated finite things which gave some plausibility to your dialectic. Perhaps, therefore, you would care to make some comments on my remarks, particularly on what I have said about your reductive analysis.'

II

In the first place I have no wish to deny that we can look on the world as a unified evolutionary process. Indeed, in the last chapter (p. 158) I expressly stated that: 'From the physical point of view the world presents itself to us as a massive system of things which are interrelated in such a way that the presence of the system is a necessary condition for the existence of any member.' And this system is a dynamic, developing system. Thus we can say, for instance, that man's existence requires the presence of the system, not simply in the sense that he depends here and now on other members (air for example), but also in the sense that his presence in the world requires, as a precondition on the physical level, the evolutionary process which preceded him.[2] My metaphysical reflections certainly do not commit me to denying any of these facts.

In the second place I have no wish to deny that we can superimpose on the foundation of physical facts and hypotheses a general interpretation of the world-process which goes beyond scientific hypotheses as generally understood and can be termed 'metaphysical'. The attempt to find a comprehensive pattern in the world process on the basis of reflection on the discoveries and theories of the various sciences is in my opinion a natural and legitimate enterprise. It is natural in the sense that man, involved in the developing spatio-temporal system but at the same time capable of reflecting upon it, is naturally inclined to ask, for example, whether it has any 'meaning'. That is to say, is it a teleological process, moving towards a goal? And the enterprise is legitimate in the sense that there may well be indications in the world-process, as presented to us by the sciences and by history, of a certain direction which suggests one pattern rather than another. Some people may wish to argue that the enterprise cannot count as 'real metaphysics'. But such a position appears to me to express an unduly narrow idea of metaphysics.

In the third place, however, I do not agree with the critic's suggestion that an interpretation of the world-process as teleological in character renders superfluous any recourse to the idea of a transcendent reality. And in the present section I wish to make some remarks on this subject.

M

A teleological interpretation of the world-process obviously involves the concept of the subordination of the whole mechanism, so to speak, of the process, to the attainment of a determinate end. The mere recognition of historical facts— for example, that in the course of cosmic history successive levels or types of being have appeared[3]—does not by itself constitute an adequate warrant for describing the world-process as teleological. For it is possible to admit the historical facts and at the same time to maintain that the lines of development which have actually occurred have taken place simply as the result of the chance fulfilment of certain preconditions, and not in view of the attainment of any telos or end. The word 'chance' is perhaps not a happy one. But the view referred to is that life, for instance, arose simply because certain conditions for its development happened to be fulfilled, and not because the fulfilment of these conditions and the consequent emergence of life were required for the attainment of a determinate end. It may be that in vast tracts of time it was highly probable that these conditions would be fulfilled. And some might wish to say that the fulfilment was 'necessary'. But if this statement meant no more than that, given the initial material and sufficient time, it was inevitable that the conditions would be eventually fulfilled, one could hardly speak of such an interpretation of the evolutionary process as a teleological interpretation. For this involves the notion of a movement towards an end or goal and of the selection of means to attain this end. Such a notion does not indeed involve the exclusion of every idea of necessity. It does not, for instance, exclude the idea that for a given level in the evolutionary process to appear certain preconditions were physically necessary. Nor does it exclude the idea that in vast tracts of time it was highly probable that the preconditions would in fact be fulfilled. But, as already remarked, a teleological interpretation of the world-process clearly implies that the whole mechanism is subordinated or directed to the attainment of an end.

Now let us suppose that someone wishes to maintain that the course of the world-process is necessary in the sense that it could not have been other than it is, and at the same time that it is a teleological process. If he means simply that the potentialities which are, or are thought to be, latent in matter must necessarily be actualised in virtue of a purely physical and mechanical causality, there does not seem to be any good reason for describing the process as teleological. If this description is to be justifiable, it must be maintained that the whole necessary process was brought into existence in order that the result, which is inevitably attained once the process has been set going, should in fact be attained. But this theory clearly demands the concept of a creative power which transcends the process itself.

The same conclusion follows if we wish to maintain the following position. The process is not necessary and inevitable throughout, but there is selection of means to an end, this selection being conscious and deliberate. For to attribute to matter in its primitive state (however we conceive this state) a conscious and deliberate selection of means to an end would be too grotesque and bizarre to possess any plausibility. It would go well beyond the limits of reputable panpsychistic theories. If therefore we wish to maintain the position in question, we shall be driven in the end to introduce the concept of a reality which acts within the world-process but at the same time transcends it. One could, of course, speak of the fulfilment of an Idea, in accordance with which certain means to the attainment of an end are selected out of the total range of possibility. But it is sufficiently obvious, I think, that if by 'Idea' we mean an eternal pattern or exemplar Idea which is fulfilled or realised in and through the world-process but which itself transcends this process, we are driven inevitably to introduce the concept of transcendent Spirit. For if we exclude this concept, what can the ontological status of the Idea possibly be?

If, therefore, we accept the imagined critic's suggestion that we can perfectly well add to the purely empirical study of the world-process a metaphysical picture which involves a teleological interpretation but which at the same time excludes as superfluous the concept of a transcendent Absolute, we must, I think, have recourse to the idea of an unconscious selection of means to an end. We must interpret the world on an analogy with the living organism, which can reasonably be regarded as displaying teleological activity and selecting means to a determinate end, though not by conscious and deliberate choice.

Probably we shall have to adopt some form of panpsychism. Infra-spiritual Nature will be looked on, for instance, as slumbering spirit, to borrow a phrase from Schelling. And humanity's developing scientific knowledge of the world can then be regarded as the world's knowledge of itself. Thus if we speak of the world-process as the Absolute, we have the picture of the Absolute coming to self-consciousness in and through man. If we speak of the process as the fulfilment of an Idea, the Idea is regarded as being immanent within the process. It is transcendent only in the sense that at no given stage of cosmic history is the Idea completely fulfilled or realised.

This picture can certainly be presented in such a way as to render it impressive. I have no wish to deny this. But difficulties arise when it is ecamined in detail. Let us take, for example, the emergence of the biological sphere. In a panpsychistic theory everything is presumably 'living' in some sense. But even if we pass over the question whether this very wide use of the word 'living' does not tend to empty it of definite meaning, room must still be found for the phenomena corresponding to what we call the emergence or appearance of life. And life did not arise everywhere in the universe. Where then is the activity of the unconscious selection to be located? Are we to say that certain molecules or groups of molecules, acting unconsciously or subconsciously for an end, brought about the conditions for the emergence of life? Or are we to attribute this teleological activity to the whole universe, representing it as creating in part of itself the conditions required for an important step (namely the emergence of the biological sphere) in the gradual attainment of the ultimate end of self-consciousness—that is, the universe's consciousness of itself in and through man? It is presumably the second alternative which fits in better with the general picture sketched in the last paragraph. But what ground have we for thinking that the universe could act in this way? It is difficult to avoid the impression that the real ground is not any objective evidence but a determination to find a half-way house between a non-teleological interpretation of the world-process and a teleological interpretation which involves recourse to the idea of a transcendent creative power. It may be said that the idea of organic Nature, animated by a world-soul, is of very ancient origin and cannot properly be represented as the result of a compromise of this sort. But I do not think that this historical remark is much to the point. For we are dealing not with ancient Greek philosophers but with thinkers who are undeniably acquainted both with non-teleological inter- pretations of the world-process and with teleological interpre- tations which include reference to a transcendent power. And it is perhaps worth noitcing that those who favour the mediating position under consideration are often apt to speak about Nature intending this or Evolution doing that, thus transferring personification from transcendent Spirit to a sphere in which its applicability is highly questionable.

It may be asked what all this proves about the world. In one sense, of course, it proves nothing at all. That is to say, it does not show what is the correct description of the world-process. My primary purpose however in making the foregoing remarks was not to argue that the world-process is or is not teleological in character, but rather to challenge the validity of the imagined critic's suggestion that we can perfectly well picture the world as a teleological process without introducing the allegedly superfluous notion of a transcendent creative reality. In my opinion at least, if we wish to add to the empirical study of the world-process a metaphysical and teleological interpretation, we shall be driven either to introduce the idea of a transcendent creative power or to make vague statements which pretty well imply that Nature or Evolution conceives an end and selects means for its attainment.

III

The reader may perhaps feel inclined to comment that by attacking the imagined critic on the foregoing lines I have simply added weight to his contention that the dialectic of reason which was adumbrated in my chapter 9 is untenable or at least superfluous. For have I not admitted that the world can be looked on as a unified process in the course of which individual things come and go? And does not this admission imply that the world cannot be reduced to separate things and relations, but that unity is prior to plurality? And even if I have not tacitly admitted that my reductive analysis of the term 'world' is untenable, does not my attitude imply that the dialectic in which this analysis forms an important moment is superfluous? For if it is true that acceptance of a comprehensive interpretation of the world-process should lead us to accept the idea of a transcendent creative power. what need is there for an abstract dialectic of the type outlined in the last chapter? After all, general interpretations or 'visions' of the world, when these are based on some plausible connection with the discoveries and hypotheses of modern science,[4] mean a great deal more to most minds than do abstract metaphysical arguments, especially when these may be accompanied by an uneasy feeling of unreality even in the minds of those who propose them.

This line of criticism is understandable. But I am not prepared to admit that my reductive analysis of the term 'world' is untenable. Of course, if one thinks of things exclusively in terms of objects such as stones, trees, animals and human beings, the reduction of the term 'world' to 'things' may seem to be naïve and untenable. For it is obvious that these kinds of things did not always exist. And if one thinks backwards into a past which stretches out far beyond the confines of human experence, one may be inclined to picture to oneself a primitive state of unity and lack of differentiation, a kind of indifference-point at which all distinctions between things vanish and are lost to view. But suppose for instance, that we think of a time when there was a countless number of infinitesimal particles. In a certain sense plurality would be more marked than it is now. After all the organism is a structural society, a system within a system, which has emerged in the course of ages. And it is just as reasonable to regard the process of evolution as a process of the creation of structural societies, a creative process of bringing together into unities, as to regard it as a process of differentiation out of an undifferentiated unity. Hence I do not think that cosmic history gives rise to any fatal objection against my reductive analysis. When it is possible to speak of a world at all, it is possible to speak of things. True, if we adopted the hypothesis that plurality originated through the explosion of some primeval entity, plurality would be genetically subordinated to unity. But in this case one would probably speak of the world originating through a primeval explosion, thereby implying that plurality, a plurality of 'things', belongs to our ordinary concept of the world.

That things form a system, that they are related to one another and are physically interdependent, I have not denied; on the contrary, I have affirmed it. But I have also asserted that though the world forms a physical system of such a kind that the presence of the system is a physical condition for the existence of any member, 'from the metaphysical point of view the world falls apart, as it were, into finite things, each of which is existentially unstable, and contingent relations' (p. 158). That is to say, no one thing, no one member of the system, implies the existence of any other member by a relation of logical necessity. Or, better, it is not absolutely impossible that any one finite thing should exist without any other finite thing existing, provided, I should add, that the originating and sustaining activities which are normally exercised by other finite things were supplied by the creative and conserving activity of a transcendent reality.[5] This position I still maintain. And it seems to me quite compatible with a full admission of the fact that the world can properly be regarded as a unified and developing system. Hence I do not believe that my reply to the imagined critic tacitly implies the untenability of my reductive analysis of the term 'world'.

Nor do I believe that the dialectic outlined in the last chapter is superfluous, in the sense that it has no useful function to perform. I have indeed challenged the validity of the imagined critic's suggestion that we can perfectly well add to the empirical study of the world-process a comprehensive teleological interpretation which excludes any affirmation of a transcendent Absolute. But to challenge a certain view by pointing out some difficulties to which it gives rise is not necessarily the same thing as to refute it. It remains open to anyone to maintain that the difficulties can be answered on the basis of the theory that the universe is itself the Absolute, a self-developing teleological unity which is in no need of a transcendent ground of existence. And it is here that the dialectic outlined in the last chapter can perform a function of great utility by destroying the world's pretensions, if one may so speak, to be the Absolute and so facilitating the movement of transcendence. It may very well be true that most of those

whose minds are open to metaphysical 'visions' expect to be
shown a pattern in the world as it is known to them by
experience and through the sciences, and that they feel that
thep are being fobbed off with 'the same old stuff' if they are
offered abstract metaphysical arguments instead. But it is not
a question of offering what I have called the dialectic of reason
to the exclusion of, say, a general teleological interpretation
of the world-process. For the two things are compatible. A
teleological 'vision' of the world-process can give flesh and
blood to the more arid skeleton of abstract metaphysics. And
one might, if one wished, try to exhibit a teleological pattern
in this process without making any reference to my reductive
analysis. But the dialectic in which this analysis constitutes a
moment performs the function of calling in question the
ultimate adequacy of the world as the ground of existence of
finite things. I say 'ultimate adequacy' because from the
physical point of view, the point of view of the scientist, each
member of the world-system has its ground of existence
immediately in other finite things and mediately in the whole
system. And the physical scientist is not concerned to proceed
any further. But the metaphysician, as I conceive him, does
proceed further. He performs the reductive analysis of the
world and proceeds to unify things on the existential level by
relating them to the transcendent Absolute as the ultimate
ground of their existence.

IV

The question still remains, however, whether the metaphysician, as I conceive him, does not simply assume that
there must be an Absolute. That he does so was one of the
imagined critic's main contentions. Reductive analysis of the
term 'world' may serve to show that the world is not a super-
entity which can properly be called the Absolute, and that
consequently, *if* there is an Absolute, it must transcend the
world. But why should there be an Absolute at all? The
assumption that there must be seems to be common both to the
philosopher who tries to transform the world into an Absolute
and to the philosopher who affirms the existence of a transcendent Absolute. Yet it is precisely the validity of this

assumption which requires to be justified. Why should it be supposed that reason has to transcend the empirical world at all? Because a finite thing must have a 'sufficient reason' or an 'adequate ground' of its existence? But everything has a ground of existence. If for the sake of argument we picture the world as an infinite series of phenenomena, A has its ground in B, B in C, and so on. Obviously, B is not the sole condition for A's existence; for B itself is dependent on C. But the 'adequate ground' of A's existence lies in the infinity of the series. For if the series is infinite, we never come to a member which is suspended, so to speak, in the air; we never come to a point at which the so-called movement of transcendence is required in order to find a ground of existence. True, the metaphysician may say that the series is not a necessary being. But he is then assuming that there must be a necessary being. If he appeals to the correlativity of the notions of contingent and necessary being, it seems that he tacitly defines 'contingent being' in such a way that the proposition, 'if there is a contingent being, there is a necessary being', becomes an *analytic* proposition which simply illustrates the use or meaning of certain symbols and gives us no extra-linguistic information. And if the metaphysician does not find empirical causes 'sufficient reasons' or 'adequate grounds' for the existence of any given finite thing, this is surely because he presupposes that there must be a ground other than the grounds revealed in experience and the sciences. True, presupposition is not perhaps an apt word. For it suggest the idea of a consciously and deliberately framed hypothesis, whereas it is more a question of an initial faith. The point is, however, that this initial faith governs all the metaphysician's thinking, all his demands and his movement of transcendence in response to these demands.

As I have allowed myself little space for my reply to this line of criticism, it will have to be expressed briefly and dogmatically. In the first place let us consider the intelligibility of being. If this is a presupposition, it is not made by the metaphysician alone. For instance, unless the imagined critic is prepared to maintain that the scientist sets out to impose a purely subjective construction on an unknowable X, he must admit that the scientist 'presupposes' the intelligibility of being. For if the opposite were presupposed, who would apply himself to scientific inquiry? To be sure, scientific hypotheses are constructions of the human mind. But they are constructed with a view to knowing the world better. Hence, if the intelligibility of being is presupposed in metaphysics, it is presupposed also in natural science. And if the presupposition is legitimate in natural science, it is legitimate also in metaphysics.

But in what sense is the intelligibility of being presupposed? Perhaps the critic would like to suggest that if it is presupposed by the scientist, it is presupposed as a fundamental hypothesis and that actual scientific development serves as an increasing verification of this hypothesis, whereas metaphysical theories cannot be verified in the same way. But it would be absurd to suggest that before the child knows anything it forms the hypothesis that things are knowable. The intelligibility of being is not a presupposition in the sense of hypothesis. If it is called a presupposition, what is meant, or ought to be meant, is that it is a condition of knowledge. It is not a condition of which the mind must be aware before it knows anything: it is simply a condition which must be fulfilled if we are to know anything. That it is fulfilled is apprehended implicitly in the act of knowing anything. Explicit apprehension is due to subsequent reflection.

The imagined critic will doubtless say that this reply does not touch the main point of his criticism. For his objection is that the metaphysician gives to the intelligibility of being a special sense and thus begs the whole question, not that he presupposes the possibility of knowledge in general. But to this I should reply that the significance of the intelligibility of being in a metaphysical context is imposed on, and not by, the metaphysician. I have already maintained in the last chapter that the understanding of things on the existential level signifies their existential unification, without conflation or obliteration of the things to be unified, and that this existential unification means the relating of the many conditioned to one unconditioned.[6] This is not a meaning arbitrarily imposed by the metaphysician—it is simply what understanding means in a metaphysical context. Hence, the choice really lies between abstaining from metaphysics and affirming the Absolute in some form.

The radical anti-metaphysician sees this, of course, quite

clearly. And if the path leads in a direction in which he does not wish to go, he is wise, from his own point of view, in arguing that there is no path but only a mass of briars. But his attempt to justify the refusal to enter upon the path by maintaining that the metaphysician, under the pressure of an initial act of faith, tacitly gives to ordinary words, such as 'explanation', unusual meanings which beg the whole question at issue is open to serious criticism. To be sure, if I ask for the explanation of a certain letter, I am not asking for the ultimate ontological ground of its existence; I am probably asking for the writer's motive in composing and sending the letter. And if I look for the explanation of the failure of the electric light, I am looking for an empirical explanation. But to say that the word 'explanation' must be used only with reference to empirical causes, motives and so on seems to me to constitute a piece of dogmatism. The imagined critic will, of course, say that I have misunderstood his position. We ask for example, for the explanation of the letter because we are already well aware through experience that human beings are not normally accustomed to write letters without any motive or reason. We therefore know that the word 'explanation' can be used in this sense. But, even if there is a metaphysical ground of existence, we do not know this through experience. Hence we do not know that the word 'explanation' *can* be used in a metaphysical sense. The metaphysician simply assumes it, and he does so under the pressure of an initial faith in the Absolute. Well, we do not, of course, experience instances of the Absolute in the sense intended. But this does not show that the meaning of the term 'explanation' is incapable of legitimate expansion. The expansion of meaning is not arbitrarily predetermined by the metaphysician and then smuggled in as it were under the cover of a word which is relevant only in other contexts; it is forced upon the metaphysician in the actual process of understanding. Ultimately the question is whether one is going to understand (in the sense already described) the manifold on the existential level or abstain from the attempt to do so. What the radical anti-metaphysician is doing is to issue a prohibition against making the attempt.

The critic will say that this is nonsense. He does not forbid understanding. What he says is that the existence of any thing is sufficiently understood when it has been related to empirical causes. And, as already observed, in an infinite series there is no point at which empirical causal explanation becomes 'insufficient'.

My reply to this is obvious from what has been said above. To understand the manifold of finite things on the existential level is to relate the conditioned to the unconditioned. Within the framework of my dialectic, reason tries to find the unconditioned in the world. But this involves transforming the world into a comprehensive self-sufficient Substance which is something more than contingent things and relations. The reductive analysis performed in the second moment of the dialectic destroys this transformation by reducing the world to conditioned things. The idea of an infinite series thus becomes irrelevant. For an infinite series of conditioned things does not make an unconditioned being: it is simply an endless chain of conditioned things. Reason is thus driven to perform the movement of transcendence, relating the conditioned to a transcendent unconditioned, a transcendent Absolute.

If therefore we consider the movement of transcendence as comprising two moments (from empirical things to the idea of the world as an Absolute, and from the destruction of this idea to the affirmation of a transcendent Absolute), it is perfectly true that the necessity of the Absolute is 'presupposed' by this movement, if by this statement we mean that the movement of reason towards the unconditioned is logically antecedent to the two moments just mentioned. But it is not a presupposition or assumption in the ordinary sense. For the direction of thought towards the unconditioned is simply the movement of reason itself in its process of understanding in a given context.

The imagined critic will probably continue to maintain that metaphysics rests on an initial assumption or act of faith. He may also maintain that I have practically admitted this, though by representing this 'assumption' as inherent in the movement of reason itself, when it attempts to understand in a given context, I have tried to avoid the conclusion that the objectivity of metaphysical reflection is impaired by an initial assumption of fundamental importance. Instead of resuming the debate, however, I wish to point out that there is little reason to suppose that we can ever reach a point at which the determined critic is unable to make this type of accusation if he so chooses. For example, I have maintained that the completely isolated finite thing is unintelligible, in the sense that reason cannot rest in this idea but strives to overcome the isolation. And I am convinced that this is the case. I am also convinced that some of those who speak of things as being 'gratuitous', *de trop* or 'just there' betray by the very phrases which they use the fact that their reason is not satisfied with the idea of a finite thing as 'just there'. At the same time, however, if someone is prepared to go on maintaining that he can perfectly well conceive of a finite thing being 'just there', there may well come a point in the discussion when one cannot do much more than offer one's interlocutor a cigarette and change the subject of conversation. It is idle to suppose that communication is possible under all circumstances whatsoever. For experience surely suggests that it is not. If there comes a moment at which the discussion has to be broken off, the critic may retain the fixed impression that the metaphysician makes fundamental assumptions and is unprepared to recognise the fact. But the metaphysician may well retain the fixed impression that the critic simply puts a bar to the movement of understanding in a certain context because, for reasons which it can be left to others to determine, he does not wish to travel along a path which, as he sees clearly enough, leads in a certain direction. When it comes to the matter of accusations, what is sauce for the goose is sauce for the gander.

A final remark. The immanent movement of reason towards the Absolute manifests the finality of the spirit—that is, of the human person as spiritual. Behind metaphysics there lies man, the being who transcends the world as involved in it and is involved in the world as transcending it. In this sense the critic has rightly suggested that metaphysics rests on a 'profound impulse'. And there is also a sense in which it can be said that all reasoning and argumentation in metaphysics is subordinate to this profound impulse. But it does not follow that the process of reasoning is void of objectivity. For metaphysics is precisely a way to the Absolute through the activity of rational reflection, the objectivity of which is not destroyed by the 'impulse' which gives rise to the reflection.

Notes

CHAPTER I (pp. 1–17)

1. *The Essentials of Logic*, London 1895, 166.
2. R. W. Newell, *The Concept of Philosophy* London 1967, 15.
3. Prologue to Book I of Ockham's commentary on the *Sentences*, question 9, *Guillelmi de Ockham Opera Theologica*, Vol. I, St Bonaventure, N.Y. 1967, 259.
4. In *Individuals. An Essay in Descriptive Metaphysics*, London 1959.
5. In *Metaphysics*, London 1963.
6. We can of course define religion according to the characteristics of what we believe to be the true religion. Or we can take a paradigm case of what is universally admitted to be a religion. A religion will then be defective in so far as it fails to exemplify our definition. But I prefer to start with a broad concept.
7. *On Selfhood and Godhood*, London 1957, 248.
8. *Issues in Science and Religion*, London 1966, 10.
9. Needless to say, I am thinking of phrases such as 'socialism is my religion'. If socialism were embraced primarily as a matter of expediency, or in a spirit of conformism with the ideas of a man's social environment, the phrase would not ring true. But if we thought that the man who uttered the sentence was governed by a social ideal which served to unify his life and activities and for which he was prepared to sacrifice himself, even his life if need be, we would know what was meant, and I do not think that we would see anything very odd in the utterance.

    Obviously such sentences as 'X is his religion' can be uttered in regard to something trivial. But then we think of them as exaggerations. Again, X may signify something which we consider undesirable or of which we disapprove. But I am doubtful whether this possibility really affects the point at issue, unless indeed we wish to claim that to call something somebody's religion is by definition to commend it. In point of fact we do not consider all religions equally good and admirable.

10. It has been said by some writers that one of the differences between philosophy and religion is that religion involves worship, which is no part of philosophy. Up to a point this seems to be true. There is an obvious difference between, for instance a Christian or a Jew reciting or singing psalms and Kant working out the *Critique of Pure Reason*. At the same time there is room for some qualifications. On the side of philosophy, we can at any rate envisage a philosopher pursuing his studies in a spirit of worship. After all he might think of the pursuit of truth, in whatever form it may assume, as a way of worshipping God. On the side of religion, Buddhism in its original form (if we describe it as a religion) does not involve what would be ordinarily thought of as religious worship. Yet it is clear that Buddhism as it has developed in history, and especially when it has been adapted in such a way as to meet the need of people in general, has certainly incorporated worship into itself. In other words, whatever may be the case with Buddhism as an austere philosophy of life, as a world-religion, adapted to the laity and its needs, Buddhism certainly lends support to the thesis that worship is an essential feature of religion. Even if religion in some sense can exist without what would normally be called worship, history suggests that this is not true of a definite world-religion or of a popular religion. However, a philosophy can be religious, even though we would not speak of it as a 'religion'.

11. *Philosophical Investigations*, E. trs. G. E. Anscombe, Oxford 1953, I, 119.

12. *Metaphysics*, 184.

13. *Ibid.*

14. *Ibid.*

15. More accurately, I suppose, it is the realisation of a value which can be regarded as a matter of ultimate concern.

16. *Signs, Language and Behaviour*, Englewood Cliffs, N.J. 1946, 148.

17. What I mean is this: in the experience of a value (for example, love) as having an overriding claim on the will, a man comes up against an 'absolute'. A man's ethical theory, if he has one, may not admit of absolute values. But I am referring not to his ethical theory but to a recognition of an absolute claim, a recognition which can show itself in various ways and which may be inconsistent with the man's professed ethical theory. It is arguable that a recognition of this kind is a response to a self-disclosure of the divine reality under the aspect of the Good. This is of course an interpretation with which the man himself might not agree. But I do not think that it is absurd to

envisage the case of someone calling himself an atheist, who, for 'human purposes', would have to be classified as such and yet would not count as an atheist in God's eyes.

18.   *Essays on Truth and Reality*, London 1914, 15.

19.   By 'old-fashioned Thomists' I mean, in effect, those who reject the method of transcendental reflection represented by Marechal, Marc, Lotz, Coreth and, in his own way, Lonergan.

20.   Professor H. D. Lewis, if I understand him correctly, maintains that there is, or can be, an intuition not of God himself but of the necessity of God, when 'God' is taken to mean ultimate reality of the Unconditioned. That is to say, Professor Lewis holds, I think, that there can be an intuitive insight into the dependence of all finite things on a reality which transcends them. What this ultimate reality is like is a further question.

It is obviously open to anyone to meet this claim with the statement that he at any rate enjoys no such intuition. And some would doubtless argue that what Professor Lewis calls an intuition and distinguishes from an inference is really a swift inference, and an invalid one at that. But it seems to me undoubtedly true, from the phenomenological point of view, that some people seem to themselves to have an intuitive insight into the necessity of an ultimate ground of finite existence. And some such belief seems to me to lie behind the classical *a posteriori* metaphysical arguments for God's existence. That there is an 'ultimate explanation' seems to such metaphysicians to be self-evident. It may also be the case that the so-called ontological argument tends to recur, in spite of all logical criticism, because the idea of God, at any rate in a minimal sense of the concept 'God', imposes itself on some minds. Indeed, Lewis says explicitly that 'in the case of God, to understand the concept is to see, in the very same thought, that there must be one instance of it and that there cannot be more than one' (*Philosophy of Religion*, Teach Yourself Books, London 1965, 147).

The position adopted by Lewis bears, I suppose, some resemblance to that of Jaspers. For Jaspers does not wish to claim an intuition of God himself. But inasmuch as Jaspers is intent on leaving room for the man who is acutely aware of the aspects of empirical reality which occasion what Lewis describes as an intuition and who none the less rejects or denies God, he always speaks of 'faith'.

21.   *Acts* 17:28.

22.   *The Evolution of Religion*, Glasgow 1899, I, 67.

23.   *Enneads*, I, 3, 1–3.

24. *Way to Wisdom. An Introduction to Philosophy*, E. trs. Karl Manheim, London 1951, 42.
25. *The Autobiography of Bertrand Russell*, I, London 1967, 187.
26. *Ibid.*
27. *The Autobiography of Bertrand Russell*, II, London 1968, 38.
28. *Philosophy and Illusion*, London: New York 1968, 93.
29. *Ibid.*
30. *Ibid.*, 32.
31. *Way to Wisdom*, 42.
32. *Appearance and Reality*, London 1899, 447.
33. *Speculum Mentis*, London 1924, 151.

CHAPTER 2 (pp. 18–35)

1. *The Value and Destiny of the Individual*, London 1913, 229.
2. See, for example, *Ideas y creencias* (1940). In Ortega's *Obras Completas*, this work is included in Vol. V (Madrid 1947).
3. Ortega was much given to thinking in terms of 'generations', each new generation being regarded as a new social body with its own historic task to perform, to which it might be faithful or unfaithful.
4. Ortega believed that to discover what genuine philosophy is we have to go back to its origins, and that it originated in a 'vital need'.
5. *Laws*, 885 f.
6. I am neglecting, of course, Aristotle's use of the terms 'theologians'.
7. It is hardly necessary to say that I am referring to the Hindu metaphysical philosophers of the old tradition of India, not to those modern Indian thinkers who have been strongly influenced by western thought, to the extent of embracing philosophies such as logical positivism or Marxism.
8. *John* 1 :9.
9. I say 'at any rate of terms' to allow for alteration in the meanings of terms when used in the theological statement of Christian doctrines.
10. Augustine's analysis of time in the eleventh Book of the *Confessions* is an example. Whether one agrees with it or not, it is a remarkable piece of work.
11. A medieval thinker such as Aquinas tended to look on the philosophy of Aristotle, as much more 'monolithic' than we are likely to do.
12. The picture of theology taking its premises from divine revelation obviously encourages a propositional view of

revelation. But there is no need to enter upon this theme at the moment.

13. The statement, that is to say, that everything which is moved is moved by something other than itself ('motion' including all change, as with Aristotle).

14. That is to say, Scotus thought of Aristotle's first unmoved mover as a physical hypothesis.

15. It is true that according to Ockham the philosopher can provide a good argument for the existence of a first or supreme conserving cause of the world. But it seems that in his opinion this conserver might be, for all that the philosopher can show, simply relative to this world. And a conserver of this world might not be at all the transcendent Creator of the Christian religion.

16. Ockham insists on the moral obligation of following conscience. Even if a man is mistaken in believing that God commands something, he is morally obliged to do it, if this is what he sincerely believes.

17. *History of Christian Philosophy in the Middle Ages*, London 1955, 498.

18. I am referring of course to the Christian medieval West.

19. *Ethics*, Book V, proposition 19, proof.

20. See, for instance, chapter 14.

21. Some expressions of the tendency to find the 'inner' philosophical truth of Christian doctrines can be found in Leibniz, and also in the writings of Lessing. As Lessing rejected the distinction between natural and revealed religion and regarded the religious history of mankind as a progressive revelation of process of divine education, he naturally rejected the distinction between demonstrable religious truths and revealed mysteries which are indemonstrable. We must add, however, that Lessing did not believe that absolute, final truth is actually attainable at any given moment. He would hardly have spoken, as Hegel did, of absolute truth. But even if, for Lessing, religious truths approximate, in varying degrees, to the absolute truth which is possessed by God alone, he evidently thought of this approximate truth as discernible by the human reason. That is to say, it was a question of seeing the intrinsic truth of a belief, not of accepting the truth of a proposition simply because it was regarded as having been revealed by God. (Lessing tended to take a pragmatic view of religious truths, making their truth relative to their effect on conduct. But I omit consideration of this aspect of this thought. It is sufficient to note that from one point of view his attitude to religious doctrines looked forward to that of Hegel.)

CHAPTER 3 (pp. 36–53)

1. *John* 14:6.
2. Cf., for example, 1 *Tim.* 2:5.
3. Willem F. Zuurdeeg, *An Analytical Philosophy of Religion*, London 1959, 136.
4. The word 'parasitic' is not used here in an emotive sense, but in the sense in which philosophy of science can be described as 'parasitic' in science itself.
5. In his article 'Religion and Science' in Vol. VII of the *Encylopedia of Philosophy* J. J. C. Smart finds several areas of tension, such as immortality and the efficacy of prayer. But particular cases of this kind cannot well be discussed here.
6. *Process and Reality*, London 1929, 18.
7. I am assuming of course that there are such contingent features. And this assumption might be challenged. However, in ordinary thinking we tend to distinguish between what could conceivably be otherwise and what could not, between what is necessarily the case (given the existence of a world) and what is not necessarily the case.
8. If one has in mind a deductive system as found in pure mathematics, it is clearly doubtful whether all such propositions can be exhibited as forming a system—as, that is to say, deducible one from another in a logical order from one indemonstrable proposition. But the word 'system' need not be used simply in this very strict sense.
9. The existence of the One, of the Godhead, can obviously be approached in different ways. For example, a philosopher might wish to argue that the existence of God is a necessary condition of the possibility of a world, of any finite thing at all, thus relating the existence of God to the logical scaffolding of the world. Duns Scotus argued in this sort of way. But I am not concerned here with arguments for the existence of God.
10. *Logical Positivism* edited by A. J. Ayer, London: Glencoe, Illinois 1959, 80. The quotation is from Carnap's article entitled 'The Elimination of Metaphysics through Logical Analysis of Language'.
11. *Appearance and Reality*, London 1899, 533. Bradley is talking about theistic philosophers.
12. Psalms and hymns often contain statements about God. But these are part of an act of worship of God. In any case they are statements of faith, rather than conclusions of metaphysical arguments.

13. Even if we take the provability of God's existence as a premise it does not follow that we have to look on one particular series of historical events rather than another as revealing the divine action.

14. See *New Essays in Philosophical Theology*, edited by A. Flew and A. MacIntyre, London 1955, 99–103.

15. Needless to say, I am not referring to believers in God who think that the best approach to modern unbelievers is to dwell, at any rate in the first instance, on aspects of or elements in religion which do not involve explicit mention of God. To be silent about God in order to speak to a man of what he can more easily understand or appreciate is not the same thing as to eliminate the concept of God from religious discourse.

16. *Philosophical Investigations*, I, 116.

CHAPTER 4 (pp. 54–72)

1. See, for example, *Alciphron*, 4, 16–22 and *Dialogues*, 3.

2. See *Critique of Pure Reason*, second edition, 667–8; *Critique of Practical Reason*, 244–6, and *Reflexionen zur Metaphysik*, *Gesammelte Schriften*, Vol. 18, Prussian Academy, 420–26, 489–500.

3. 'God spoke to Moses' is a factual statement, whereas 'I baptise thee' is what J. L. Austin called a performative utterance. 'I believe in one God' is, on the face of it, an autobiographical statement. But when uttered in the liturgy it obviously possesses other functions than giving information about the speaker's beliefs. For instance, it has a self-commitment function.

4. Antony Flew, *God and Philosophy*, London 1966, 43.

5. We could hardly examine the evidence for the existence of a black swan, unless we knew what the term 'black swan' meant. And the concept of a black swan is in principle capable of a plurality of instantiations. But the concept of God, as understood in Christianity, Judaism and Islam is the concept of a being which is necessarily unique.

6. Some eastern thinkers have regarded being and not-being, for example, as not mutually exclusive and have remained unworried by what they regarded as trivial objections on the score of the demands of logic.

7. H. P. Owen, *The Christian Knowledge of God*, London 1969, 192.

8. *Thought and Action*, London 1959, 233–4.

9. *Summa contra Gentiles*, I, 30.

10. By 'term' I understand of course what Ockham called the *terminus conceptus*. I mean the word as significant, not as a *flatus vocis*.

11. *John* 4:8.

12. *John* 14:6.

13. For example, if it is said that God is transcendent, the statement has to be qualified in such a way that it does not exclude the divine immanence. But this qualification is an explanation of what we mean when we say that God is transcendent, or, if preferred, what we do not mean.

14. *Letter* 56, to Hugo Boxell.

15. *In librum De Causis, lectio* 6.

16. *Ascent of Mount Carmel*, Book III, ch. 12, section I.

17. *Ibid.*

18. *The Story of My Heart*, with an introduction by Elizabeth Jennings, London 1968, 51.

19. I am aware of course that existentialism is a portmanteau word. I am also aware that some philosophers who have been commonly classified as existentialists have repudiated the label. But I use the word here to cover the philosophies which are commonly classified in this way.

20. Heidegger does not regard himself as an 'existentialist'. But Bultmann uses what we may describe as the existentialist elements in Heidegger's thought. Bultmann's Heidegger may be somwhat different from Heidegger's Heidegger. But this does not alter the fact that Bultmann has derived stimulus and ideas from this source.

21. As Sartre regards the idea of God as self-contradictory, he cannot be justly accused of simply begging the whole question from the start.

22. This phrase occurs in *L'être et le néant*, Paris 1943, 708. The general idea is that man's basic effort or striving is to be God, i.e. being in itself and being for itself in one. The idea of this synthesis is the self-contradictory idea of God (self-grounded conscious being).

23. The argument involves the assumption that consciousness (*le pour-soi*) is not-being, a privation of being. This notion seems to me indefensible, not least in view of the activity which Sartre himself ascribes to consciousness.

24. *Situations*, I, 153.

CHAPTER 5 (pp. 73–91)

1. I am thinking, for example, of the experience or feeling or sense of sublimity and mystery in Nature. This can involve at any rate the feeling of Nature as manifesting a 'presence', the presence of that which is hidden and probably not conceived in any definite or determinate form.

2. William James suggested that God might act on the subconscious or infra-conscious.

3. In *Mysticism and Philosophy*, Philadelphia and New York; London 1960.

4. See *The Transcendence of the Cave*, London 1967, 202.

5. *Enneads*, VI, 9; II, 771 b.

6. *The Two Sources of Religion and Morality*, E. trs. by R. A. Audra and C. Brereton, with the assistance of W. Horsfall Carter, London 1935, 216.

7. Bertrand Russell, *Wisdom of the West*, London 1959, 293.

8. In '*Bergson on Morality*' (*Proceedings of the British Academy* Vol. XLI) I criticised the philosopher's ethical theory. But though I am not a disciple of Bergson, I think that he has been undervalued in recent years.

9. It is easy to talk about phenomena 'making better sense' in one world-view than in another. But what is meant by 'making sense'? And what are the criteria for deciding whether something 'makes sense' or not?

   If a given statement asserts what is logically impossible, it is safe to say that anyone who recognises this logical impossibility will be prepared to allow that the statement does not make sense. But if it is a question of different possible interpretations of a set of facts or data, a man's judgement about which makes better sense obviously depends to a large extent on his presuppositions. Given my high estimation of Tom's character, it makes better sense, as far as I am concerned, to interpret a certain action which he has performed in a sense favourable to Tom. But for someone who does not share my high esteem for Tom another interpretation might seem to make 'better sense', an interpretation unfavourable to Tom.

   Perhaps therefore we come back again to the question whether there are criteria for deciding between general world-outlooks or 'bliks'. Given theistic premises, certain interpretations naturally tend to make better sense than certain other interpretations. But is it not the case that to say that they make better sense is to say that they fit better into a certain pre-existing framework? This may well be true. But then we need some way of discriminating between frameworks.

10. Some theologians insist that to see X as such-and-such is not to make an inference. If this thesis is applied in the present context, it means that mystical experience in particular, and perhaps religious experience in general, is or can be seen as manifesting divine action, without any inferential process. But the theologians in question make the revelatory character of events correlative to faith. That is to say, the events manifest God to the eyes of faith. And if this is applied to religious experience, it follows that there would be little point in using religious experience as a datum on which to base an *argument* designed to convince agnostics or atheists. For what can an argument be but inferential? However, one might draw attention to mystical experience in the hope that this would provide an occasion for the awakening of a faith for which the occurrences would be revelatory.

Another difficulty is that the term 'religious experience' can be used to cover a good many types of occurrences which the Christian at any rate would be unlikely to regard as revelatory, in the sense of manifesting the divine action. Where do the principles of discrimination come from? What would make a Christian see experience X as revelatory and experience Y as non-revelatory (in the sense mentioned)? It is presumably pre-existing beliefs which provide the basis for discrimination. For example, God is believed to be of such a nature that certain experiences can hardly be regarded as manifesting divine action. The atheist, however, does not share these pre-existing beliefs.

11. Perhaps these should be distinguished. For we might wish to regard a general conceptual scheme as giving expression to a world-vision. But we might also regard the world-vision as taking shape and concrete existence in so far as it is articulated in a conceptual scheme.

12. It may be asked why we should adopt the criterion of comprehensiveness. Well, it is precisely an overall conceptual scheme which, *ex hypothesi*, is being looked for. It can also be argued that there is a natural desire to obtain conceptual mastery over as wide a range as possible of phenomena or of different types of human experience.

13. I use the word 'persuasiveness', as it is difficult to see how a comprehensive world-vision can be proved in such a way as to leave no room for reasonable doubt. Let us assume, for

instance, that a theistic world-view is better able than a naturalistic world-view to accommodate religious experience. There still remains the 'problem of evil', which becomes an acute problem precisely within the framework of theism.

14. Frederick Ferré, *Basic Modern Philosophy of Religion*, London 1968, 353.
15. *Ibid.*

CHAPTER 6 (pp. 95–111)

1. Some people object to this label, quite unnecessarily it seems to me. As the term 'linguistic' or 'logical analysis' is used here, it signifies an approach to and way of doing philosophy rather than any set of philosophical dogmas.
2. G. J. Warnock, *English Philosophy since* 1900, London 1958, 145.
3. Some English philosophers tend to speak as though they had a monopoly of modernity. But unless they make this true by definition, the continental existentialists are just as modern as they are.
4. Gilbert Ryle in *The Nature of Metaphysics*, edited by D. F. Pears London 1957, 160.
5. The use of the term 'why' obviously differs in these two cases. In the first case it means 'for what reason?' or 'with what motive?', while in the second case it probably means 'what was the efficient cause?'.
6. This is, of course, the view associated with the name of Wittgenstein.
7. Cf. J. J. C. Smart in *New Essays on Philosophical Theology*, edited by A. G. N. Flew, and A. MacIntyre, London 1955, 46.
8. L. Wittgenstein, *Philosophical Investigations*, London 1953, I, 115.
9. *Ibid.*, I, 122.
10. *Ibid.*, I, 122.
11. *Contemporary British Philosophy*, Third Series, edited by H. D. Lewis, London 1956, 489–90.
12. *Ibid.*, 489.
13. P. F. Strawson, *Individuals, An Essay in Descriptive Metaphysics*, London 1959.
14. Mr Strawson's idea of revisionary metaphysics can obviously be connected with Dr Waismann's idea of original metaphysical systems as embodying different 'visions'.
15. *Individuals*, 9.
16. *Ibid.*

17. It is significant that the term 'conceptual analysis' has tended to become common in recent years.

18. I do not mean to commit myself to acceptance of the adequacy of this distinction. But, given the line of approach, it is a natural distinction to make. And it obviously has an objective basis.

19. A. J. Ayer, *Language, Truth and Logic*, London 1936, 2nd edition 1946. Though not representative of the climate of contemporary British thought, this book is a classic in the sense that it is an extremely clear and forthright expression of a particular brand of philosophy and for this reason possesses a lasting value.

20. *Individuals*, 9.

21. I do not forget my admission that the metaphysician may receive his preliminary guiding idea or initial 'vision' from religious belief. But I prescind here from such considerations in order to concentrate on the movement of the mind common to speculative metaphysicians, without reference to their antecedent beliefs.

22. *Contemporary Philosophy: Studies of Logical Positivism and Existentialism*, London 1956, 227.

23. *Philosophy of Religion*, Introduction, A.2,1.

24. *Contra Gentiles* 3, 25.

25. L. Wittgenstein, *The Blue and Brown Books*, London 1958, 18.

26. *Ibid.*

27. Wittgenstein remarks that 'Not *how* the world is, is the mystical, but *that* it is '(*Tractatus Logico-Philosophicus*, 6, 44).' As I have said elsewhere (*Contemporary Philosophy*, 73), one might substitute 'metaphysical' for 'mystical' at least to indicate the emphasis of metaphysics.

28. *De intellectus emendatione* I.

29. Wittgenstein, *Philosophical Investigations*, I, 126.

30. M. Heidegger, *Sein und Zeit*, Halle a.d.s. 1929, 1.

31. M. Heidegger, *Was ist Metaphysik?*, Frankfurt a.M. 1949, 38.

32. J. P. Sartre, *L'être et le néant*, Paris 1943, 713.

33. Somewhat paradoxically perhaps the atheistic existentialists, through the conclusions which they draw from atheism, set the importance of the problem of God in clear relief.

CHAPTER 7 (pp. 112–126)

1. *A Treatise of Human Nature*, I,4,6.

2. *Ibid.*, Appendix.

3. The theory has, of course, been expressed as a linguistic theory, but I am considering here the frankly ontological statement of it.
4. *Ethical Studies*, London 1927, p. 39, n. 1.
5. *Tractatus Logico-Philosophicus*, London 1922, 5.633.
6. *Ibid.*, 5.632.
7. *Appearance and Reality*, London 1889, 81.
8. All this raises the question of the dynamic structure of the human personality and of the relations between the distinguishable levels. For a treatment of this question one can recommend *The Soul in Metaphysical and Empirical Psychology* by Stephen Strasser, Ph.D., Pittsburgh: Louvain 1957.
9. 'The feeling of the world as a limited whole is the mystical feeling', *Tractatus Logico-Philosophicus*, 6.45.
10. *Tractatus Logico-Philosophicus*, 6.44.
11. *Essays on Truth and Reality*, London 1914, 16.

CHAPTER 8 (pp. 127–144)

1. *Contemporary Philosophy: Studies of Logical Positivism and Existentialism*, London 1956, 61.
2. *Ibid.*, 62.
3. *Op. cit.*, 61–2.
4. *Ibid.*, 61.
5. *Ibid.*
6. I do not wish to refer by name to any philosophers who write in this way. For I am interested only in the theme. And I desire to avoid any appearance of personal polemics.
7. *The Function of Reason*, Princeton 1929, 29.
8. *Process and Reality*, London 1929, 3.
9. I do not mean, of course, that the human spirit can know its relationship to God only through metaphysics. But I am prescinding altogether from revealed religion and supernatural faith.

CHAPTER 10 (pp. 161–177)

1. Questions about the existence of pure finite spirits and their relation to 'the world' need not concern us here. I regard angelology as pertaining to theology rather than to philosophy.
2. These remarks are certainly not intended to imply that the human spirit can legitimately be interpreted as a mere epiphenomenon, the existence of which is adequately ex-

plicable solely in terms of physical preconditions. But the fact remains that on the physical level human existence presupposes the world-system.

3. I use the ambiguous word 'appear' because I wish to pass over controversial questions about the origins of particular levels and to make a historical statement which would be accepted by all.

4. I am thinking, for example, of the evolutionary hypothesis, especially when it allows for novelty, the appearance of something new.

5. This remark should be interpreted in the light of the context, and not as a statement of deism.

6. Obviously the existence of things could not be said to be fully understood without knowledge of their end. Hence, though I prescind here from final causality, it would be more accurate to say that the relating of finite things to the Absolute as ground of their existence constitutes part of what is meant by understanding them.

INDEX

The letter n. followed by a number, indicates a reference note.